CW01628971

*To my Dad, Davie…*
*Look what your little girl has gone and done.*
*This book would never have been written if it weren't for you.*
*It took losing you for me and Donna to realise what we had to do.*
*We know how proud you would be.*
*Thank you from the bottom of our hearts.*

# BECOME THE REAL YOU

THE PRACTICAL LIFE GUIDE TO DITCH SELF-DOUBT, STAND IN YOUR POWER & STEP INTO THE BEST VERSION OF YOU

DONNA ELLIOTT & CHERYL LEE

authors AND CO.

**Disclaimer - No Medical or Personal Advice**

The information in this book, whether provided in hardcopy or digitally (together 'Material') is for general information purposes and nothing contained in it is, or is intended to be construed as advice. It does not take into account your individual health, medical, physical or emotional situation or needs. It is not a substitute for medical attention, treatment, examination, advice, treatment of existing conditions or diagnosis and is not intended to provide a clinical diagnosis nor take the place of proper medical advice from a fully qualified medical practitioner. You should, before you act or use any of this information, consider the appropriateness of this information having regard to your own personal situation and needs. You are responsible for consulting a suitable medical professional before using any of the information or materials contained in our Material or accessed through our website, before trying any treatment or taking any course of action that may directly or indirectly affect your health or well being.



ISBN13: 978-1-913728-45-8

# CONTENTS

# FOREWORD BY NIYC PIDGEON

> **"Inner peace (peace of mind, personal peace):** *a deliberate state of psychological or spiritual calm despite the potential presence of stressors such as the burden arising from pretending to be someone."*

I was interviewed for a magazine recently and the journalist asked me, *"Niyc, what's the best thing about being a successful entrepreneur...?"* I didn't need to think about how to respond to the question because I was already very clear on my answer: *"Being able to wake up every day and just be myself, no matter what I'm doing."*

Whether I'm rolling out of bed to go to my workout, stepping on stage to speak in front of thousands, in my office writing books, meeting with my team, or going out to dinner with friends, I'm always the same person, and it's something I don't take for granted.

Being able to be yourself is a concept so simple, and at the same time so incredibly complex when you consider what we need to do to simply feel comfortable showing up as ourselves.

Behind the scenes that might mean discipline, and dedication, and going places inside yourself that you've potentially never opened up to explore. It might look like getting intentional about your happiness, pushing outside of your comfort zones, and having a good hard look at what things aren't working for you.

As an award-winning positive psychologist, best-selling author, and certified coach, I've made it my life's work to help people live with more joy, personal power, and unstoppable success within themselves and their lives. Rather than seeing this as a goal somewhere out there in the future, I understand it as a process that is ever unfolding – an adventure within which we get to meet ourselves every step of the way.

The beauty of honouring this process, and learning to know, love and trust yourself, is that you get to experience the richness of life on so many levels. You'll find yourself raising your awareness, opening up new opportunities, shifting your thinking, deepening your understanding, becoming more bold and more tender at the same time, as you expand your horizons and start to welcome in more of *The Real You.*

It's a journey we are all honoured to have available for us – and you must consciously choose it. Most of the world still doesn't know what personal development is, let alone embrace it with open arms. Because you're here reading these pages my intuition is that you have a sense of knowing inside of you, a knowing that is guiding you to be, do, create and have so much more.

*And it always starts, with you.*

In this book, **Become The Real You**, you're going to drop into a new understanding of what happiness really is – and where you can find it too. You'll discover how to understand your own feelings and behaviours, gain clarity on who you are, and will leave armed with the tools to make better choices and to keep you feeling empowered, vibrant, and like all things are possible, no matter what's going on in your day.

Having known and worked together with Donna and Cheryl for years now, I've been witness to who they are and how they truly live what they teach. Trust that the words you read in this book are words poured onto the pages from their hearts, with love, wisdom, expertise, and the highest vision for your growth and good.

Not only am I thrilled to see this work brought to life because of the mission it helps to further and fulfil, but I'm also thrilled to be in the celebration of two amazing women from the North East of England, who have claimed their place in our world, got to know themselves, and shown up to create an outstanding example of results, paving a way for so many others to do that too.

Remember, your power doesn't come from outside of you, it's already within you – and there's infinite possibility available for you when you start to connect more intentionally inside with your own self first.

No matter whether you're feeling on top of the world right now, you feel nervous with anticipation, or you're actually having a really bad day – just take the first step right now in reading these pages and get curious about where the path might lead for you. Let go of the attachment to the outcome, and let's enjoy the journey together along the way.

My hope, my wish, and my invitation for you, is for you to take the opportunity this book offers you right now with both hands, grab it, and run with it, as if your life depended on it.

Because the fact is, in so many ways, it actually does.

With Gratitude,

Niyc Pidgeon

**Positive Psychologist MSc IPPA, Hay House Author "Now Is Your Chance", Certified High Performance Coach, Founder of Unstoppable Success, & Positive Psychology Coach Academy Certification.**

** Source, Wikipedia*

# INTRODUCTION

> *"What we need are women who are full of themselves. A woman who is full of herself knows and trusts herself enough to say and do what must be done. She lets the rest burn."*
>
> — GLENNON DOYLE, UNTAMED

Life does not have to be one long hard struggle and then you die. There's so much more that is possible for you. There is so much opportunity to live your life in a bigger way than you are right now, but you know that a lot of the time, that lack of confidence in what you bring to the table, that lack of belief that you are enough, stops you from going for the life you *really* want.

You weren't born to be fucking mediocre and to play small to keep everyone happy. So let's agree right now – that ends here, today.

You've been wearing all of those masks for so many years that you actually forgot who you are. We want you to wake up and have you live your very best life by becoming your true self.

We want you to get unstuck from the day-to-day crap of busy to-do lists and connect with what you want from this life, get out of your own way and become the best version of you.

You see, we know you didn't really mean to get stuck, it just sort of happens. Our life shapes us: our childhood, our experiences (good and bad), the setbacks, the challenges, the conditioning, the traumas, the labels we give ourselves and the ones from others – they all form part of our *identity*. The thing we believe ourselves to be. You're playing the part, performing in various roles without even realising that you're doing it. We form all of these stories and beliefs about ourselves and the world around us. They keep us paralysed, keeping us 'safe' where we are, as it's what we know.

As women we want to make everyone else around us feel good, so along the journey of life we give away little pieces of ourselves to please everyone else. We give so much away, we love and care so much for others, then one day we wake up and we don't recognise who we have become. We aren't even sure when it happened, but we find ourselves in lives we feel so disconnected from. We aren't unhappy but there's something missing.

You know that you're not living to your full potential: you're lacking purpose. You feel like you're meant for more…

But you don't admit that. Hell, no!

That would mean that you're being selfish, greedy and dismissing your life. That would mean that you're not grateful for the life you have and the people in it. So you keep on with the busy lists, on that hamster wheel of life, going through the motions... safe in your daily business. Quashing those thoughts of 'more' whenever they pop up.

Just like we did for all of those years, believing that it wasn't possible for us.

It's a big fat lie.

It *is* possible for you.

Whatever 'it' is.

That whisper within you does not and *will not* go away. It will become a roar.

And our biggest fear? It's that you spend your whole life ignoring it.

We each spent over twenty years as people leaders in our corporate careers before we set up our business, Now Is Your Time, and created *The Real You*™ which is our signature coaching methodology. We were both obsessed with developing people, but we never really took ourselves seriously enough to set up a business doing it until we were in our forties, for reasons which we will share as you go through this book.

Let's be clear – there's nothing special about us. We don't have magical powers or some secret formula to life that you don't have. But we do have a shed load of life lessons and a willingness to speak openly about them, coupled with a combined half century of coaching people.

We were blessed that our careers led us to each other and since we met many moons ago, we have been best friends and Soul Sisters who have a shared passion for helping people to see themselves as we see them – *capable of anything.*

Our wish for you is that no matter how quiet your whisper is right now or how big the roar, you take the journey with us as The Universe has already guided you to this book – and *that* tells us that whether you know it or not ...you're ready.

You're ready to work out what your real purpose is.

You're ready to understand what's blocking you.

You're ready to move through it and *Become The Real You*.

The happiness, balance, confidence, success, abundance, grace, ease, joy, fulfilment, purpose... all the good stuff. It's all there and available to you right now. No more waiting.

All you need to know is how and that's why we are here with you today. We invite you to allow us to be your Guides, your Coaches, your Cheerleaders and your Accountability Partners.

This journey will show you how to think better, because everything that you've manifested in your life so far is a result of your thoughts. When we want different things in our lives, we start with learning how to think differently. As Mindset Coaches, we believe that when you master your mindset, you master your life.

> *"The only impossible journey is the one you never begin."*
>
> — TONY ROBBINS

This is how you'll get the most from this journey and this book:

- Don't just read this book, DO this book. Be an active participant rather than a passenger. You learn best by doing. When you get to your *Time To Keep It Real* sections, go *all in*.
- We have created free Book Resources to support you

which you can download from www.therealyoumethod.com/book-resources - they're going to bring this experience to life for you.

- It's the perfect excuse to break out the fancy stationery, so treat yourself to a new journal or grab the one from the drawer you've been waiting for a special occasion to use. This is it!
- Make this book your Life Guide. Turn corners over on pages that you love, underline parts that resonate with you, scribble your notes in the margins. It's the highest honour for a book to be loved that way!
- In each chapter you can make a note of your biggest 'aha' moment. We love to hear them so email us at hello@nowisyourtimeto.com and tell us what they are.
- Share your fave lessons from the book on your socials and make sure you tag us @nowisyourtimeto – it makes our day when we see you learning, growing and seeing you become *The Real You*.

Let us show you how we did it, how our clients are doing it right now. Our best life and mindset strategies are here in this book to empower you to live *your* happiest, most expansive, most fun and fulfilled life.

And we promise you, whilst there may be some tears as you release what no longer serves you, there will be so much more fun along the way.

Now Is Your Time to Become *The Real You*.

We are ready. Let's do this.

Donna & Cheryl xx

# 1

# BECOMING

> *"In order to rise from its own ashes, a Phoenix first must burn."*
>
> — OCTAVIA BUTLER

**Donna**

It was about 9pm on a Friday evening in winter and I was standing in my bedroom with two bottles of pills in my hand. All of this trouble, the upset making everyone I loved around me crazy, and I was the epicentre of it all. It was down to me that all of my family were stressed out. My friends were worried sick. The only one who seemed unaffected was the dog. But I knew that someone would take care of him. If I just disappeared then all of this shit would go away with me.

I had already ruled out running away. Let's face it, you have to have money to do that. And as the judge had already pointed out, my divorce was, "The worst financial quagmire ever seen," so running away to an exotic island (or a Premier Inn in the UK) was just not an option. I barely had enough money for my food.

Divorce. That word made me feel like such a big, fat failure. I had made my bed and had to lie in it. People in my family didn't get divorced. I couldn't be the first. It was like a giant public admission that I hadn't been able to fix him, that I hadn't been enough. What would everyone think? The shame of that, of having everyone look at me and wonder how I hadn't even been able to hang on to someone who slept around and assaulted me, had kept me in that marriage for seven years. I preferred to stay in a marriage where I was beaten and emotionally manipulated than tell the world that I hadn't been able to make it work. Whilst he spent the money I earned and conned countless women into affairs with him, I kept a lid on it all.

I showed up each day as a happy, smiling, bubbly person. I had a great career and an amazing family, so there was no sense in letting them know what went on behind closed doors. They wouldn't believe it anyway. I was strong, independent and career driven – or so I had everyone believe. I was so disgusted with what I had become that I could only imagine what everyone else would think of me. It didn't bear thinking about. I couldn't even look at myself in the mirror without wanting to vomit. At least this way, wearing my mask and armour every day with a big, idiotically empty smile on my face, meant it was only me that had to endure it.

It was fucking exhausting.

I placed the bottles of pills on the tallboy and I felt anxious about how devastated my Mam would be and I was working through who might find me. I didn't want that to be unpleasant for them, so I was trying to think how to not cause them more distress than there needed to be. I thought to myself how strange it was to be thinking so calmly, so practically and to be stone cold sober all at the same time. Yes. Me not being here anymore would just make things easier for everyone and they would be able to move on with their lives. It was enough now.

I heard my front door open and seconds later, there was my younger sister, Kelly, standing in front of me in the doorway to my bedroom.

"I have no idea why, but I felt like I had to be here," she said. As she looked at me with her huge green eyes, I could feel the worry emanating from her in waves. She had no clue what was going on in my mind but something in her knew that something was off. For some reason, she had turned up at my door, let herself in and come straight to the bedroom to find the woman that she had always called 'her Rock' standing, suspended in thought.

It's hard to describe what happened inside of me next.

All I can say is that I knew she was sent to me. Something, a voice inside said to me, "You're ok, it's all going to be ok."

In that moment, a sense of relief washed over me. Like someone had clicked their fingers and I was released from a spell and was beautifully jolted back into the land of the living as me, but different.

I know how crazy this all sounds, but it was instantaneous. Now I believed in Angels.

For the first time in longer than I could remember, a quiet stillness settled in me, a knowing.

*I was going to be ok.*

"Is everything ok? Donna?" She sought reassurance from her big sister, avoiding asking me if 'I' was ok...

"Yes."

And I meant it.

2

# FINDING YOUR POWER AGAIN

> *"Turn your wounds into wisdom."*
>
> — OPRAH

Hand up if you're a control freak? Ours is raised and we reckon it's a pretty safe bet that yours is too. We all work very hard at having our life be a certain way in order for us to enjoy it. That usually involves having the ones we love safe and happy. Smashing it at work or in our business. Earning enough to enjoy nice things and have great experiences. Eating well. Working out. Being super organised. Having the house always looking good... the list goes on.

When all that stuff is as it should be, *then* we can relax, chill out and be happy.

That is where the glitch lies in your plan.

When you do this, you are always putting your power to be happy, content and in harmony with life in the hands of something that's *outside of* your control. Then happiness and harmony are only available to you when all the other ducks are lined up – and you're not the one responsible for the ducks! You may *like to think* you are but let's face it... other people have their own minds. Irritating as that is and as much as you probably love to think that you're The Boss Of Fucking Everything like we do – people are going to do what they want to do and life is going to do what life does and it hasn't always read the script that you have written for it.

> *"If you cannot find peace within yourself, you will never find it anywhere else."*
>
> — MARVIN GAYE

Making your inner glow and peace of mind contingent on life doing exactly what you want it to do is how you are giving your power away every day, over and over again.

## FEELING POWERLESS

The number of ways in which we can feel powerless are immeasurable. As self-confessed control freaks, feeling powerless isn't a good place to be. When we feel we are losing our grip, we then try harder and harder to take back our control so that we feel like we are back in the driving seat.

Here are some of the ways we felt powerless in our lives along with examples that some of our Soul Sisters in our coaching programme, *The Real You,* have shared with us:

- Scared that I don't know who I am any more
- My partner just takes me for granted

- I'm always worrying about money and sick of never having enough
- I've sacrificed so much for this career and now I'm not sure it's what I want
- My job has me trapped; I can't leave because I'm in golden handcuffs
- The kids aren't making the right decisions about their future
- I gave up my dreams for my family and now I don't know what to do next
- I'm being made redundant and am worried there won't be another job
- I never have enough time to get everything done
- I'm always trying to lose weight and am constantly in a yo-yo diet cycle

We dislike feeling powerless. We are trying desperately to get back that semblance of having all of our shit together so we try twice as hard, through gritted teeth and with dogged determination. We grasp and claw our way through until we come out the other end... bruised, battered but generally quite chuffed that we pulled it back from the brink. We feel like we are hurtling from one life drama to the next, waiting for this mystical point in life when everything settles down so that we can finally start to really kick back and enjoy it. Then we can stop controlling and just be.

Newsflash. *That ain't ever going to happen!*

Life is about enjoying all of it. Feeling powerful through all of the highs and lows. Experiencing the agony and the ecstasy. It's about contrast and that isn't going to stop no matter how hard you or we try to control it. Accepting, embracing and welcoming that will be a massive win for you and will give you back a heap of energy that you won't be wasting on trying to control everything outside of yourself. You're going to start getting real and getting accountable for the circumstances of your life and you're going to feel so much lighter, freer and empowered because of it.

> *"Be happy for no reason, like a child. If you are happy for a reason, you're in trouble, because that reason can be taken from you."*
>
> — DEEPAK CHOPRA

---

### TIME TO KEEP IT REAL

Ok, time to reflect on what came up for you so far. Take some space and answer the following questions. Be as real as you can with yourself to create powerful shifts.

Where are you feeling powerless?

Where are you trying to control?

Where do you desire a shift in your reality?

---

**Donna**

I remember the first time that I read that we have to take accountability for the stuff that's happened in our lives – the good, the bad and the ugly. "ARSEHOLE!" I screamed at the author and slammed the book shut. I was responsible for being a punchbag for my adulterous ex-husband for years? That was all my fault?! No. Fucking. Way.

After that night when my sister walked into my bedroom, I set about working out who the hell I was. How had I become this woman who had lived for years making herself ok to be in a relationship where she was emotionally and physically abused? What had happened to me, that I had so freely given away my joy and right to laugh without being punched in the face? When had I become so lost that the thought of not living this glorious life had become a consideration? What the hell was so wrong with me that everyone in the world thought I was this intelligent, strong, high-performing woman who could show up at work like everything was peachy, but it was all just a sham, a fake ID of me pretending to be her?

I was determined to find answers, not to why my ex-husband was what he was… I knew that answering that wouldn't change anything for me. What I had to work out was who *I* was, what was going on *inside of me* that I had allowed the events that had taken place to happen and to keep happening over the course of our relationship.

Don't get me wrong, I went through the phase of hating, blaming, raging against the injustice and horror of it all. I had worked hard for years to build the facade that was my life and now everyone knew what was really going on. I was mortified. I was ashamed. I was devastated, especially when I found out that I would potentially go bankrupt and could lose the home I had worked so hard for – that was for sure a low point. But even while I was in it, I was aware that it didn't feel good to feel that way. I knew being in that heightened state of emotion was hurting me and me alone.

---

"The breakdown comes before the breakthrough."
*Donna & Cheryl*

---

Feeling a victim, as if I had no say in what had transpired, absolutely terrified me. That, to me, meant that it could all happen again with someone else if I ever got into another relationship. That wasn't a path I was willing to walk down. It was time to dig... deep.

## YOUR BS – BELIEF SYSTEM

I couldn't get this line out of my mind about taking accountability. It jangled my nerves so much that I knew I had no other option but to sit in my discomfort and explore it. There had to be a reason it was pushing my buttons *so* hard. I decided to play the game with an open mind and a willing heart. I wanted to know how to be something other than I was and I was building myself and my life from the ground up. I realised that I had nothing to lose in trying.

What I learned about myself was this:

- I had ignored my intuition which had told me that something was off right from the start
- I closed my eyes when I saw the flashing neon signs telling me to listen to my gut
- I pretended the big red flags weren't there
- I denied the mountains of evidence which had told me from when I met him that I should run in the opposite direction, including people actually warning me about him
- I had given my power away repeatedly and tried to pretend it wasn't happening

Due to this, I had made some pretty shitty, head-in-the-sand, naive decisions and *that* was what I had to get accountable for. There had been a million opportunities for me to take a different path but I chose to stick to the one I was on. I had found a reason and excuse for each marker I passed which was pointing me in the direction of safety and chose instead to buy into what he was telling me. And that was because his version aligned with some of the big beliefs I had about myself back then.

> *"Nothing binds you except your thoughts; nothing limits you except your fear; and nothing controls you except your beliefs."*
>
> — MARIANNE WILLIAMSON

Your beliefs are things that you accept to be true. They are ideas about yourself and the world that you hold as fact. Because of this you tend not to question them and for the most part, you're not even aware that they are there. Yet they are, and they're running the show that is your life every single day. Super brainy scientists tell us that you have around 60,000 thoughts a day and of those thoughts, around 95% come from the part of your mind where all of these beliefs hang out – that's your subconscious mind.

We aren't going to bombard you with a ton of stats but this one is important. This means that 95% of what you do each day is coming from the part of your mind that is a pre-set programme of the beliefs that you have wired in there. Doesn't that blow your freaking mind? And doesn't it explain A LOT?

One of my big beliefs back then was that it was my job to fix people. I even called myself, 'The Fixer!' No matter how broken, I believed it was my job, my responsibility, to make them feel good about themselves again. Whatever the cost may have been to me personally.

---

"You are not your beliefs, your thoughts or your feelings."
*Donna & Cheryl*

---

## YOU AND THE UNIVERSE

Now we need to explain something else at this point. The Universe is like this infinite, all-knowing love machine who always wants so much for you to be happy. To the extent that she says, "YES!" to everything you ask for and she is always tuned in to you, always waiting for you to share what it is that you're ready to call into your life. Think of the story of Aladdin and the Genie of the Lamp – that's The Universe. Ready and waiting to take your order. You are basically one gigantic magnet. You're always radiating your unique vibration and telling her what you are ready to receive.

And get this...

Your vibration comes from your feelings... and your feelings come from your thoughts and your thoughts come from... you guessed it – *your beliefs*!

There I was back then, *believing* that I could fix people and clearly sending out that vibration loud and clear because what I kept getting in my life was a string of men who needed some fixing. "Hey, guys, I'm over here! If you want help with your drug problem, here I am! Abandonment issues? Yes, of course, they're welcome too! What's that? You struggle to be faithful and you have trouble committing? Oh, my God yes, of course, I can totally cure you of that. Come over!"

The Universe was matching my vibration and doing her job giving me exactly what she *thought* I wanted. Until I did this digging to find out how this had happened, I had no idea of how powerful I was, that I was actually creating these scenarios in my life. I want to be really clear about something here. I'm not saying that I blame myself for violent behaviour towards me and I'm certainly not saying that I was responsible for his actions. But I was responsible for my own decisions and for me, understanding where I had lost my power and why that had happened was critical so that I could claim it back and start to rebuild my life and trust myself.

What I learned was that until we change our belief systems, until we change who we believe we are and how we see ourselves, then all we are ever doing is basically putting lipstick on the pig. Not the nicest expression, but you know what we are getting at! If we keep tinkering around with the results of our thinking as they manifest in our lives, then we are only ever going to get different versions of what we currently have. Nothing will significantly change until we do the deeper work of changing our thoughts and in order to change those, then we have to rewire, reset and reprogramme our beliefs.

---

"Your belief system is being mirrored back to you
by what's showing up in your life."
*Donna & Cheryl*

---

This is how we create ourselves from the inside out. We go right to the very identity of who we are, of who we *believe* we are, and then we get to decide who it is we want to be and we declare it into existence. You get to be and embody whomever you consciously choose.

## WALKING BACK TO YOU

Through this book as you walk this journey with us and do the work to rewire your beliefs, you will totally change the game for yourself because you're going right to the root of the problem. You're going to take out the first domino which starts the chain of events.

Think of it like this.

When you go to the doctor, they give you medicine to help the symptoms of what you have so they improve. The problem keeps recurring and you keep going back to the doctor because each time you're a bit more cheesed off that it's happening. Eventually, the doctor sends you to a specialist for some further diagnosis. He runs more sophisticated tests on you, involving scans and such and he then identifies the cause of the issue and can then recommend a different cause of action. One that will treat the cause and stop the requirement for the pain medication from the doctor.

This is exactly what happens when you make the decision to do the work on your beliefs, on your mindset. You're going straight to the crux of the issue, right to the mothership. No messing about, straight to the main control panel to press some big red buttons. These beliefs are running the show and we want you to get very conscious about what's playing out in your life, to know where to go and how to make the internal changes necessary to have the life you dream of manifest before your very eyes.

---

"Your belief system is what's running the show."
*Donna & Cheryl*

---

You may want to go back to a time when you felt happier than you do now. You may want to be happy for the first time in your life. Either is ok, because this is *your* journey and it's already happening and it is beautiful. Don't wait for it to start. It's happening as you read this very sentence. Your life doesn't begin at the end of this book. Feel powerful right now in this very second! Here you are in this miracle moment, expanding your awareness, learning, creating.

---

## TIME TO KEEP IT REAL

Take some deep breaths and ground yourself in thanks for this moment, right here and now.

Hold gratitude and appreciation for all that you have been and for all that you are yet to become.

Take a few moments and just be and allow any emotions that come up for you.

---

## HOW DO I GET MY POWER BACK?

We are going to be showing you in this book how to find your way back to you, *The Real You*. We will be using some of the key strategies we use in *The Real You* coaching programme – which is our signature methodology that has changed the lives of so many incredible women, showing them how to reclaim their power and live their life as the highest version of themselves. We are going to take you through the key steps to change your way of thinking. The great news is that same transformation is available to you too!

We are taking the best of what we have learned over the last two decades of our lives to give you some of the most effective mindset techniques and life strategies to transform your mindset.

> *"The wound is the place where the light enters you."*
>
> — RUMI

As you go through this book and do the growth work when you're invited to, you're going to learn how to:

- Take your life experiences and turn them into life lessons
- Work out what you want to get from your life
- Identify the limiting beliefs that are in the way of that and how to rewire them
- Understand what Imposter Syndrome is and how you can break free from it
- Finally start listening and dialling up your intuition
- Create more energy so you feel high vibe all the way
- Implement the daily practices so you're living as your highest self
- Have The Universe as your bestie for the ride

We have so much we want to show you, and our belief in you and what's possible for you is off the scale. That's because what we are sharing with you isn't just theory. It's from the heart and it's the stuff that we know has the biggest impact on our clients all over the world when they apply it too. We have learned from the best and we are committed to empowering you and the other women in our movement to be the highest expression of themselves and to go at life like there's no tomorrow.

We have taken our most painful life experiences and turned them into something breath-taking.

Right now you're here because you want that change and no doubt you want it pronto. Your life didn't get this way overnight so remember to be patient (we know, we know, it's a bloody big ask) but trust the process and just enjoy getting to know *you*. This is the most important, most rewarding and most insightful relationship in your life. So lean in, get curious and above all, give yourself zero permission to skip the growth work we give you in the *Time To Keep It Real* elements.

## CHAPTER SUMMARY

- When you place your reason to be happy outside of yourself, you give your power away.
- Life won't ever be perfect so learn to enjoy it in all its messiness.
- Empower yourself by taking accountability for your part in your life lessons.
- Your Belief System is what's running the show so get curious about what is in there.
- The Universe loves saying 'YES' to you so get clear on what you're asking for.
- Learn how to use your life lessons to turn your wounds into wisdom.

**My aha moment from this chapter is:**

# 3

# YOU DESERVE TO BE HAPPY

> *"You have everything you need for complete peace and total happiness, right now."*
>
> — DR. WAYNE DYER

One of the most powerful questions we ask our clients is, "Are you happy?" and the most common response we get to that question is a long pause, a look of dismay and then lots of tears.

"I'm not *un*happy…" is often the (teary) reply.

It's the question they have been avoiding asking themselves, as once it's out in the open and it's real and they realise that actually, whilst they may not be *un*happy they're also not truly happy… then they have to *face* it.

Sometimes it's so much easier to just breeze through life in denial, pretending that everything is 'ok' and making do with a '*fine*'. In our experience 'fine' usually means Frustrated, Insecure,

Neurotic and Emotional. It's not a word we want you to use when describing your one and only experience in this body.

You see, we tend to go through life believing that full on happiness isn't realistic or entirely possible for us and certainly not every day! That's just greedy, right? We convince ourselves that daily happiness only happens to a few select people (celebs and the like) and we tell ourselves that they are probably faking it anyway so that we feel better about our own 'ok' and 'fine' existence.

---

"Being happy isn't the same as not being unhappy."
*Donna & Cheryl*

---

**CHERYL'S YOGA MAT REVELATION**

I was on a business retreat in L.A., staying in a mansion (don't hate me) with other female entrepreneurs, and whilst there one morning, I was doing Kundalini yoga. Now I can't tell you this without sounding cliché, but I had the biggest epiphany whilst on that mat. It was like a lightning bolt and that realisation was... I am spiritual.

I couldn't wait to tell Donna! I called her as soon as I could and shared my big news.

"Christ. How much are we paying for this trip? I already know that!" she laughed.

Ok, so maybe it was only a revelation to *me*. But it felt *huge*. If you had told me I was spiritual just a couple of years before that when I was in my corporate role, I would have thought you had been drinking with your lunch. Let me tell you why.

> *"The spiritual path – is simply the journey of living our lives. Everyone is on a spiritual path; most people just don't know it."*
>
> — MARIANNE WILLIAMSON

I thrived on being the best version of myself. I was a high achiever, excelling in any role I turned my hand to. I *loved* getting recognition for the great job I was doing and this spurred me on to continuously develop myself and seek out new opportunities.

When the offer of funding for me to gain a bachelor's degree came from my leader, I snapped his hand off as this would be another way to prove to everyone (including myself) how good I was at my job.

Now I have to mention at this point that I was also a single parent to my daughter, Hollie, which I had been most of her life. Balancing a senior position with lots of travel, a degree and being the only parent for my daughter was a *lot*! I didn't see this, though. I was blinded by the burning inner need to prove how together I was, how I could do it *all,* which gave me the motivation I needed to power through and just keep going.

I also loved to hang out with friends and when Hollie went to stay with her grandparents it was an opportunity for me to have an almighty blow out. I became crazy, fun time Cheryl, always entertaining everyone with my antics and being the last one on the dance floor – well, actually the last one swinging around the pole! It would not have occurred to me to take the chance of the parent-free hours to rest and recover and recharge my batteries. I got so used to flying around at one hundred miles per hour with cortisol pumping through my body, that it became my 'normal' state.

I was always smiling, glass half full, Mrs Positive, seeing the good in any situation.

If anyone had asked me if I was happy, I would have said, "YES!" before they had the chance to finish the sentence... *but was I?* If I had been truly happy, would I have been constantly looking for evidence to prove how good I was? Would I have been in a permanent state of stress, always looking for the next thing and not living in the present moment, if I were happy?

Let's face it, I was so busy I didn't even give myself the chance to stop and reflect and ask myself the question. I was often referred to as 'The Duracell Bunny' – you know, that bunny on the TV ads who just keeps bopping about when all the other bunnies have passed out. That was me. I was blissfully unaware that this lifestyle that I had created was pushing me to breaking point. Even The Duracell Bunny only has so much battery power before it falls over.

Looking back now, I'm not even sure that I knew what that *was*. I certainly didn't wake up every morning with a huge smile on my face like I do now. I was on a really fast fairground ride spinning round and round, having moments of fun and laughter, but fuck, it was *knackering* after a while and I had *no* idea how to get off.

Spiritual, *my arse*.

I had a long journey ahead to become the woman on that yoga mat, feeling super blissed out, bursting with gratitude, living her best life and serving women all over the world.

## HAPPINESS IS A CHOICE

You hear yourself saying, "I'll be happy when... it's the weekend / when I get that pay rise / when the kids are a bit more independent / when I have some savings in the bank..." and the list goes on.

Happiness doesn't have to be conditional. It isn't something you get from anywhere. It is a *state of being* that you choose to have. It's a way of living. It's a way of thinking. A way of feeling. *You have the ability to choose to be happy in any given second of your life.* How amazing is that?

And you can't use it all up. It doesn't run out or expire. The Universe doesn't have a maximum limit on how many people can be happy at any one time – it's not like a doorman at the nightclub where people start getting turned away because it's full up. There's total abundance with it and a never-ending stream of happiness is available.

> *"The key to happiness is being happy by yourself and for yourself."*
>
> — ELLEN DEGENERES

Happiness starts within. It's that warm, fuzzy feeling inside you. A sense of peace and harmony in your heart. It's that feeling of contentment with yourself and your own company. It's not about having stuff, material things like job titles, relationship status or cash in the bank to give you that good feeling. It's that sense of wholeness and fulfilment. Mind, body and spirit feeling truly aligned, connected and in flow.

We know this to be true now as this is how we feel every single day. Ok, maybe not every minute of every day but we can hand on heart tell you that you can experience true happiness every day. If it is possible for us, then it is possible for you. There's nothing available to us that isn't also available to you too.

**Cheryl**

I didn't wake up one day and decide to get off the fairground ride, choose to be happy and go skipping through the meadows, living happily ever after. It was an accumulation of life events and decisions that led me to that point – and a little bit of help from her ladyship, The Universe. It took time, discovery and a yoga mat in L.A. to show me just how far I had come from that adrenaline-junkie-crazed girl. And actually, like for you, the story started *way* before I started my career...

---

"Happiness is an inside job."
*Donna & Cheryl*

---

## MISSING PIECES

I was adopted when I was three weeks old. My parents decided after having two boys that they wanted a daughter to complete their family. Along I came with my big green eyes, brown skin and a huge mop of black hair.

I grew up in a predominantly white neighbourhood and was the only brown girl at my school. I had a different colour skin to all of my family and friends. Somewhere along the line I formed a belief that I was *different*. I had no idea this was what was going on at the time. I wasn't consciously aware I had formed this as a belief until much later in life after a lot of soul searching. As a kid, I went about my life pretending that I was the same as all the other white kids I grew up with – and they kindly reciprocated.

Fast forward to my thirties and I still didn't have a clue how much this belief was running the show... then I found NLP.

NLP, which is Neuro Linguistic Programming, is a practical modality which focuses on understanding your thoughts, language, habits and behavioural patterns. It helps you to communicate on a much deeper level and gain an understanding of how we all have our own view of the world depending on our experiences, values and beliefs. It helps you to focus on what you want to have happen in your life and to use your imagination to make it a reality. It demonstrates that if someone else can do something – whatever that is – then you can too.

I didn't realise until I started this journey the extent to which I was broken, but I was. Into tiny little pieces. I had no awareness of the huge void that existed in my life that I was constantly trying to fill. Up to that point, I was lacking self-acceptance... I didn't feel worthy or good enough. I didn't know who I was at an *identity level*. It was a shock because I always held myself to be highly emotionally intelligent, but here I was, with a truck load of scary stuff right in my blind spot.

Fuck.

> *"The only thing that will make you happy, is being happy with who you are."*
>
> — GOLDIE HAWN

One day I was in a session and I had a massive aha moment in which I became consciously aware, as a grown woman – for *the first time in my life* – that I had not yet accepted myself, my whole self, and wasn't able to love myself just as I was. I had not yet experienced *true* happiness. Shit!

This was a monumental moment because it shook me to my core. I had always considered myself a super confident, highly authentic person. And here I was grasping the reality that I didn't even know *who I was*, let alone have self-acceptance.

My journey to self-acceptance and *true* happiness started there and then and is something I consciously work on every single day.

We share these moments of our lives with you as we want you to become consciously aware of the pieces of you that may be missing right now. You may find that you are seeking validation from others so that you feel better, like I did, or you may find yourself acting the part to fit in, like I did for all of those years. You may be sitting there feeling like you would love more happiness in your life and you are unsure of where to start. You may have realised that you have some missing pieces that you want to fit together so you feel whole.

> *"Happiness comes from you. No one else can make you happy. You make you happy."*
>
> — BEYONCÉ

We want you to know what true happiness looks and feels like for you. To recognise it and not accept less than this each day so that this becomes your new daily norm.

## TIME TO KEEP IT REAL

Take ten minutes now to reflect on what we've covered in this chapter and answer the questions below. Think on them or journal them out – whatever feels good to you.

What came up for you regarding your happiness levels?

What does true happiness feel like to you?

What are you making your happiness conditional upon?

Which piece is missing for you and stopping you from experiencing true happiness?

---

**PLEASURE AND PAIN**

Life for us now is so different to how it was when we had corporate careers. I mean, we don't want to sound smug here, but life is pretty bloody awesome and we are going to share why because years ago, we didn't *believe* this would have been possible for us. We thought the whole 'live your purpose' was a bit of an urban myth, to be frank. Our reality was that we hadn't actually met any women from backgrounds like ours who were living 'the life' so to speak. In working class backgrounds in the North East of England, you grow up with a fixed view of how life should be.

It goes a bit like this:

You work hard in school and get some qualifications.

You get a good job, hopefully one for life – and you stay there.

Get married and have kids at some point.

Work hard, keep working hard and if you're lucky, have a nice holiday once a year.

You spend your whole life getting excited for when you retire, and then you can relax. Just for a bit. Before you die. That's your reward.

We personally always found it really quite depressing that you spend your whole life working hard, earning money for other people, so that you can retire *and then* start to enjoy life. Hopefully, all the hard work doesn't kill you before then so God willing, you get to the retirement element of the programme.

No thanks.

Yet we didn't allow ourselves to really go into the fantasies of having our own business. It would pop up but we would shut it down because it was a pointless waste of time. Honestly, it felt sickening thinking about it because it was like looking through a shop window full of all these delicious fancy French cakes when you're on the pre-holiday diet.

> *"The tragedy of life is not death but what we let die inside of us while we live."*
>
> — NATIVE AMERICAN PROVERB

Maybe 'one day' we would have our own business together outside of corporate life. We always said 'one day' we would come together and make a difference in the world. Then we didn't follow it up or make any plans... it was just words, handed over to The Universe as a wish.

People, generally speaking, aren't big fans of change. It feels like a lot of work and it makes us uncomfortable. We like things to be familiar because that feels safe for us. When change does come, it is usually driven by one of two things.

1. Pain – you want to move away from something
2. Pleasure – you want to move towards something

The one with the biggest punch is the first. Pain. We tend to have more motivation to change something in our life because we don't like where we are. It propels us to do something different.

Think of your health. You'll start a health plan because you hate how you feel in your clothes or are terrified to be seen in a bikini. You say things like, "I feel uncomfortable in my own skin."

Or what about your career? How often have you moved because there was just a great opportunity in a new company? Have you usually moved because you couldn't stand The Boss any more or they changed your working hours and it didn't fit in with the family?

In relationships, you often separate at the point where you can't take it any more and you can't stand to be in the same room as your partner rather than feeling like it's time to move on because the future feels brighter elsewhere.

## UNIVERSAL BITCH SLAP

For us the same was true. We had both got to the point that we were so burned out with our corporate careers, so exhausted from restructures and redundancy cycles and years of dealing with draining office politics (and don't get us started on people talking about pushing the envelope, picking low hanging fruit, optimising performance, touching base, deep diving... what the fuck is all that about?). Let's just say it was no longer bringing either of us joy.

Then Davie, Cheryl's Dad, died.

Even though he had been sick with a terminal disease, it was a shock.

This life changing event jolted both of us to our core.

*What the fuck were we doing!?*

This was the loving, spiritual bitch slap around the face from The Universe that we needed, demonstrating to us loud and clear that this is *not* a dress rehearsal. Wishing for 'one day' is a luxury and not a strategy that anyone wanting to make the most of their life would apply. And that's exactly what we had been doing. Pissing around, allowing ourselves to be 'not *un*happy' and choosing to be safe with nice salaries and playing in our zones of excellence... and not in our zones of genius.

There had been so many signs for us from The Universe over the years telling us that there was more joy available to us, but we ignored them. Actually, it's more like we didn't even see them. We were too busy putting our big girl pants on, rolling up our sleeves and cracking on. They were signs like being told over and over by friends, "You really should be a Coach, you would be amazing!"

---

"Listen up, because The Universe is always standing at the ready with a spiritual bitch slap."

*Donna & Cheryl*

---

Like you, we were going through life day to day spinning around on the hamster wheel of hustle, pushing through, accepting that the career we had was our lot and just getting on with it. How often do you take time to stop, look up, take stock, reflect, challenge the status quo... and to ask if this is the life we *really* want to be living and if not, what would we love to spend every single day doing?

Talk about playing Russian Roulette with life.

This is the deal.

Past this breath that you're taking now, nothing is guaranteed. Nothing.

We had always said that we were the kind of girls who played all out, wouldn't die with regrets – but we realised that we had made some big compromises with our lives.

We decided right there, just a week after Davie's funeral, that we were going *all in*.

## LIVING IN YOUR PURPOSE

The biggest compromise we had made was not living our purpose. We both knew that we loved coaching people and when we decided to go all in, we weren't holding back. For too long we had been ignoring and suppressing the deep longing we both had to be full time coaches. Right there and then we decided we wanted to build a global online coaching business showing women how to change their mindset, deal with their Imposter Syndrome and become the best version of themselves.

When we first sat down in HQ (what used to be Donna's kitchen) and started to develop our idea, we didn't have a clue if *anyone* would be interested! The plan was to share our life experiences and life lessons with the world – blowing the lid right off – by talking about what women were *really* dealing with and to show what's possible when you find self-acceptance.

But we were so passionate about sharing our stories of how we went from having low self-worth and not feeling good enough, to being happy with who we are and embracing all of our imperfections... and we figured if we helped *one woman* to stand in her power with confidence and self-belief about who she was then that would be worth it.

> *"Find out who you are and do it on purpose."*
>
> — DOLLY PARTON

That same week, we wrote our signature coaching framework, *The Real You*. We still have the original piece of paper we sketched it all out on! This is the backbone of our group coaching programmes which have shown hundreds of women how to live their lives as their beautiful, authentic selves.

Back then we didn't have a clue where to start or what would happen, but we knew that we weren't prepared to spend another year saying, "One day..." and that now was and always is the best time to decide to be happy and to take inspired action to go for your dreams. So there really wasn't another name option.

Now Is Your Time was born.

We had blown the lid off the jar and there was no putting it back on again! From that moment on we had this feeling of *knowing*, of certainty, that this was our purpose. That this was what we were meant to be doing. To go out into the world and be brave and vulnerable, talk about our wounds and scars, and we aren't going to lie, sometimes it felt pretty uncomfortable – it still does because we share *real* stuff!

Once we realised this was our calling it became less about us and how we felt and more about the millions of women we wanted to serve. The women like you who may be sitting there feeling 'fine' and lacking clarity and direction. Pretending to live your best life to anyone looking in, when really you feel lost, stuck and worried that this is it... then feeling waves of guilt for wanting more – *like we did for many years.*

It became our mission to show you that no matter how much shit you have gone through, how many huge frigging curveballs are thrown your way, there is a way forward. You can find *The Real You* and live life on purpose, feeling happy every day, doing what you love. It's possible for you too.

Fulfilled. Happy. Grateful.

Today we are driven by pleasure, by our mission, rather than by pain and wanting to escape and be free of something. We have got to tell you, it feels so much better.

---

"Choose today, not one day."
*Donna & Cheryl*

---

As we sit here sharing this with you today, we have helped thousands of women across the world overcome their limiting beliefs and find their confidence and self-belief to live life as their true selves. By living the fullest expression of our lives, we hope to inspire other women to do the same.

All of the answers are within you and this is about finding them, exploring them and growing into them, so you can work out what *your* purpose and what the best version of you looks like.

## TIME TO KEEP IT REAL

Maybe you already know your purpose but you're not living it or maybe you're starting from scratch.

Perhaps you have a whisper that you've been scared to acknowledge.

Now Is Your Time to get curious and lean in and to help you we have created something in your Book Resources to support you.

Head over there now before you go further and do the inner work on Discovering My Purpose - you'll love this one!

www.therealyoumethod.com/book-resources

After you've done that, come back here and write down your purpose.

It doesn't have to be perfect, that's not the goal in this book. It just has to be real and make you feel *alive*!

My Purpose is...

We hope now after reading this chapter that we have planted a seed in your mind, a seed of happiness, of fulfilment, of hope. As you continue your journey in this book, we will help you to water those seeds and turn up the brightness of your inner glow. Remember, *whatever* you desire is possible and waiting for you!

---

"What's meant for you will never go past you."
*Donna & Cheryl*

---

**CHAPTER SUMMARY**

- Being not *un*happy doesn't mean you're happy and Fine is an F word.
- Happiness is a choice and is available to you at any given moment. It's an inside job.
- Self-acceptance and self-love are necessary for us to be happy and live as our authentic selves.
- The goal isn't to work really hard, enjoy retirement, then die – it's to live your life on purpose and experience as much joy as possible.
- You're driven to make change by pleasure or pain.
- The Universe is always at the ready with a spiritual bitch slap to get you on track.
- Living your life on purpose is a total game changer and will bring you more joy than you can imagine.

**My aha moment from this chapter is:**

4

# WE ARE ALL A LITTLE FUCKED UP

> *"What makes you different or weird, that's your strength."*
>
> — MERYL STREEP

**Cheryl**

It was a week since the funeral of my Dad, Davie. I had spent the week wallowing in the house in my teddy bear onesie, binge watching Game of Thrones. Donna told me she had an idea, so I dragged my ass along the seafront road to HQ.

I sat in the sunshine in her back garden and had that first face to face chat since the funeral. I felt like my get up and go had left the building, which was a strange feeling for me as I'm happy and positive most of the time. After dissecting Game of Thrones Donna hit me up with her idea.

"I've been thinking..." she said. Now anyone who knows Donna, knows that's a bad sign! It would usually indicate that there's some work coming next!

That was when she hit me with the idea of having a global online business empowering women. I mean, I was a "Hell, yes!" right there. The weird thing is that *nothing* about it seemed weird. It felt like the absolute right thing to do.

Her idea that we were going to show women what was possible for them – to create a safe space where they could talk about what was really going on for them under the big smiles and armour-like clothing – meant that we would have to lead by sharing *our* stories.

"We have to talk about all the shit we have dealt with, how we turned our lives around." I nodded as she said this. I was already in.

"I haven't really had any bad stuff happen to me, though..."

I remember the look on Donna's face. She was trying hard not to say something.

She asked me to go home that night and list all of the tougher times in my life and she was going to do the same, make a list of the highs and lows that really stood out to us.

The next day we reconvened at the kitchen table and shared our lists.

## LIFE LESSONS

We had pretty long lists! Between the two of us, we covered adoption, infertility, divorce, single-parenthood, burnout, grief, serious money issues, abuse, family separations, imposter syndrome... the list went on!

I really couldn't get my head around how much we had gone through collectively and the mindset work we had done over the years to get to the point where we were right now. I came to the realisation that if we could have gone through all of this trauma and come out the other end, then anyone can.

---

"We have all experienced trauma."
*Donna & Cheryl*

---

But we aren't talking about it!

We all go to work, show up every day for our families, friends and colleagues with these big smiles, talking about how 'fine' everything is, when in reality most of us are dealing with something at any point in time, but we worry so much that if people really knew then they wouldn't like us or they would think less of us.

And most of us lack self-belief and security in our sense of who we are to be able to show up every day as our authentic selves – *The Real You.*

For me, when we started talking about my low points just the day before, I genuinely didn't think I had any. It's funny how you somehow forget a lot of the things that you've gone through, some dealt with and some maybe not so much. I had received a lot of coaching and done a huge amount of work on myself through my NLP qualifications over the years and knew that I had this really extensive mental toolkit that worked for me every day.

*But that's not the average story.* Most of us have had to just build a bridge and get over it. Life takes over; it doesn't slow down or stop because something has happened to us. So we suck it up, take a deep breath and put an even bigger smile on – reassuring the world that we are still 'fine'. We tell ourselves that we are 'fine' too and we want to believe it. It's way more acceptable to us than sitting in the discomfort of these deep feelings of unhappiness, helplessness or sadness, for example. Who wants to sit in that? Nobody wants to sit in their own shit!

We sweep it aside. We create this giant lump of crap under the carpet because out of sight, out of mind, right?

If only it were that easy. All of these stored up, unprocessed events carry with them strong emotions. When we store up these events by simply locking them away and throwing away the key, hoping that the skeletons in the closet stay dead, we are simply creating a backlog of emotional baggage that we are unwittingly carrying around with us. This heavy load gets dragged into every experience we have whether we are consciously aware of it or not.

Not talking about it doesn't mean it's not affecting you.

It doesn't mean it's not impacting your decisions.

It doesn't mean it's not negatively affecting your self-confidence, self-belief or self-worth.

The lugging it around impacts your life every single day in ways you will find hard to imagine and the *not* consciously dealing with these life events is holding you back from all of the happiness, love and inner peace that is available to you, to everyone. It's our hope for you that you take these *life traumas* and turn them into *life lessons*.

## YOUR SUBCONSCIOUS MIND

Your mind is a complete genius. It's powerful beyond measure. When all this stuff is happening to you, it's recording it all and storing away the memories of when you were hurt, happy, surprised, scared, lonely... you name it. Most of the thoughts you think each day actually come from the part of your mind that is on autopilot. This is your subconscious mind. All of your habitual behaviour sits here, like brushing your teeth, driving your car, breathing... all the stuff you don't have to put any conscious effort into thinking about in daily life.

It can process more information than the biggest computer known to man, so when it senses you being in any kind of danger, upset or anything that might make you scared or unhappy, it's going to kick in with memories of what that felt like earlier in your life – one of these life events – and before you know it you're behaving in a way you often don't understand.

> *"I don't associate with people who blame the world for their problems. You are your problem. You are also your solution."*
>
> — MELISSA MCCARTHY

When these events happen to us (and they don't have to be big, major things, it can be anything that's left an emotional imprint on you at the time) we put a label on ourselves. A belief is created that takes root in our subconscious mind which then becomes a part of that daily habitual behaviour. And remember, we don't think about that behaviour. It's completely in our blind spot. These beliefs about life, relationships, and ourselves can be good or bad but more often than not, the ones which are causing us the problems and getting in the way of our goals are the negative, *limiting* beliefs. Beliefs like this about the world and who we are in it, stop us from achieving the life we want to live when they're not in line with who we truly are and who we desire to be.

The reason it's so important that we talk to you about this and you totally get this point is that we don't want you to pick up this book and just do all the nice-to-do, surface level, fun stuff. We would be short-changing you if we did. For real transformation to occur, we have to go deep. Our goal for you is that you create lifelong change and have the tools to repeat these results whenever you want to go on your life journey. We could just give you lots of positive, motivational stuff and get you all fired up and ready to go – but the best houses have strong foundations. That's what we are building here with you. Clearing out all the rubble, doing all the proper groundwork and due diligence to make sure that your mind – *which is the house that you actually live in* – lasts a lifetime and can weather any storm.

## TIME TO KEEP IT REAL

Now it's time to do your rubble clearing and take a look at what lies beneath for you in your Life Inventory.

This is deep work you're going to do and we want you to clear some time and space to do this work justice.

You may be tempted to skip this exercise as it is deep, but you will use the insights from this activity as you work through the book, so it's best to do it now.

Go somewhere you can sit undisturbed with your journal and take inventory of all of your life's highs and lows. Make a list of both and notice any themes and emotions that are still coming up for you. Observe any recurring patterns.

This exercise is hands down the one that clients in *The Real You* programme find the most cathartic of all and when they also experience the most aha moments.

You've been guided to this point so have faith in the process.

MY BIGGEST TAKEAWAY FROM THAT EXERCISE IS...

## LIMITING BELIEFS

Let's get real. We are all kind of fucked up. We are all walking around with mental, emotional and sometimes even physical scars. Most of us have been traumatised by our parents at some point. We are yet to meet someone who hasn't had a shitty break up. Many of us didn't have as much fun at school as you read about in an Enid Blyton novel (showing our age!) and in general let's be honest – life has kicked most of us in the crotch on more than one occasion. And that's totally ok. It's 'normal', whatever the hell that is, but on average, most of us have experienced conditions in life that have created within us some limiting beliefs.

You can hear limiting beliefs come through in the negative things that we say to ourselves (usually in our internal chatter) every day. Sometimes we outwardly voice them too.

You know the ones. Such as...

- I don't deserve it
- I'm scared of success
- I'm not fit enough
- I'm not confident enough
- I don't have enough money
- I know people wouldn't take me seriously
- I'm not qualified enough
- I don't add any real value
- I'm a crap parent
- I'm a shitty partner
- I'm no good at sports
- I know other people are doing it better than me
- I'm not smart enough
- I'm useless with technology
- I have a rubbish memory
- I am hopeless with money
- I always make a mess of things
- I'm stupid
- I'm no good with numbers
- I am rubbish in interviews
- I'm not normal
- I'm damaged goods
- I'm so unlucky
- I'm unlovable
- I always screw things up

- I can't say no
- I always get rejected
- I don't fit in
- I'm shy
- I'm lazy
- I'm too much for people
- I'm not appreciated
- I'm a failure
- I'm not qualified enough
- I'm ugly
- I can't speak in front of people
- I'm a workaholic
- I can't have it all
- I have no boundaries
- I'm a people pleaser
- I'm disorganised
- I have no patience
- I drink too much
- I can't control my food
- I can't deal with confrontation
- I'm always late
- I'm a negative person
- I'm too old
- I'm not worthy

And the big one… the one that sits under most of these beliefs is...

*I'm not good enough.*

## TIME TO KEEP IT REAL

Take a long hard look at that list. We could have written another two pages. These were just the ones off the top of our heads, the ones we hear every single day from women we speak to.

Go through the list again. Get a pencil and tick or circle the ones you know that you say to yourself regularly. Have we missed any?

Note here the key negative / limiting beliefs you say to yourself every day.

We are going to be talking to you a lot more as we take this journey about limiting beliefs. Right now, we just want you to start tuning in to these thoughts and these words because they give you a huge amount of insight into what's going on in that gorgeous mind of yours.

> *"Any thought of discomfort or stress is an alarm that lets you know you're believing an untrue thought."*
>
> — BYRON KATIE

## JAPANESE KNOTWEED

Over the years we have coached thousands of women (and a fair few men) and the limiting belief of 'I'm not good enough' is the one that crops up time and time again.

It lies there, dormant, and pops up in many ways, shapes and forms during our life and can lurk around in our subconscious mind creating waves of unrest that we deal with in our daily lives.

Here are some of the ways that shows itself:

- Many of us have a void that we try to fill with other people's approval
- We strive to make things perfect
- We have a ton of guilt for taking time for ourselves
- We work 20% more hours than we are required to
- We assume everyone is judging us
- We compare ourselves to others
- We struggle to ask for the pay or fees we deserve
- We are uncomfortable with demonstrating vulnerability
- We feel insecure in our relationships
- We think we have to know everything
- We have a need to prove ourselves constantly
- We have blowouts of food and alcohol to feel good or not feel at all
- We don't respect our bodies and hate how we look

These are just some of the common themes we see with our clients in *The Real You*, the symptoms of the real biggie which is the pervasive feeling of not being good enough. It has a very deep root and is like Japanese Knotweed – a devastatingly dangerous weed that causes costly damage to its surrounding environment as its root system grows rapidly and damages the foundations of anything it touches. And this particular belief is often recurring and can rear its head each time you are up-levelling in life, in your career, in a new relationship or when you're under pressure in some way.

---

## TIME TO KEEP IT REAL

Where is believing you're not good enough showing up for you?

How is it limiting you?

---

## LET'S RIP OFF THE HANDCUFFS

From doing the Life Inventory, you may well have some insight into where your limiting beliefs have come from but it isn't essential right now to know exactly the moment in time they were formed. It's more important at this stage to become aware of them so that you can start the process of rewiring your mind with the new beliefs that are going to set you up for a much happier life. The fact is that the vast majority of the belief system you're currently operating with was given to you by the time you were about seven years old.

You are absorbing information, energy and starting to create your own reference points before you are even born! As you grow up, in order for you to learn all the stuff you need to know up to the age of seven, you're just recording information. Not only what you're experiencing but also what's going on in the environment around you... it's all soaking into that sponge-like mind and it's accepted as fact. There's no reasoning or bargaining – it is taken really literally and that's what has formed not just how you see the world but also how you believe the world sees you.

What you see, hear and witness going on in the home with your parents and siblings. The friends you have and the goings on at school. The TV and media. Family and community. Everything that's going into those evolving brains and accepting minds is developing an intricate web of understanding so that we know how to function in our society and quite simply as a human being.

It's mind boggling how much information you have to learn to make it safely to adulthood! Why is this important? Because you could have generated your limiting belief at any point over those years from any one of billions of different experiences so we don't want you getting sucked into only trying to work out where it came from and why you have it – right now we want you simply to commit to doing the work to embed and use only the beliefs that are going to serve you in getting from wherever you are now to where you most want to be.

However you got the beliefs you currently have, it's your responsibility to do the work to upgrade, reset and imprint *only the ones* you want to see take shape as tangible results, in your life right now.

---

"Don't talk shit about yourself - your subconscious is always listening."
*Donna & Cheryl*

---

To live your biggest life, you need to focus on turning down the volume of those limiting beliefs and pumping up the volume of the *empowering beliefs*. Having this awareness of the beliefs that are keeping you in handcuffs gives you the freedom to make a bold and liberating decision to rip those handcuffs off and set yourself free! Then you will see that the world really is yours for the taking.

## SEEK AND DESTROY

At a networking event we were introduced to Kirsty. She was fascinated by the fact that we had become Coaches after a long career in corporate and asked us for a chat where she enrolled as a One-on-One client. Her corporate career was doing really well and she was clearly highly regarded by her company, but she had an itch to scratch about whether or not it was the right path for her.

“What would you like to do?” we asked her.

“I don’t know!” she answered, clearly frustrated and a little panicked. She was terrified that she would never know and would go through her whole life feeling like she hadn’t put her finger on it. We see this with almost every new client who wants to ‘find’ their purpose.

“You *do* know,” Cheryl reassured her calmly. Because it's true. We always know, we just need a little help to get out of our own way so we can see clearly.

The thing is, the limiting beliefs are like fog in the way of your clear line of sight. For Kirsty actually it was a hill. She wasn’t sure what was at the top of it as all of the excuses (fuelled by her Belief System) were fogging up her vision. As we started to work with her to help her see what was at the top of this hill, she realised that she wanted to work as a consultant helping people in their businesses somehow, but she said she wasn’t qualified enough. She had known all along she just couldn’t accept the revelation because of the massive limiting beliefs standing in the way.

She saw herself at the bottom of this huge winding path snaking its way around a high hill. In her mind, she had created the story based on her Belief System of not being qualified enough and therefore not feeling good enough to ask people for money in exchange for that service, that she would need to study for at least ten years to become qualified enough to work in this field.

Then she thought it probably wasn’t worth doing as that was a long time and it would be challenging whilst working full time and raising a family. Her fear was telling her that she probably wouldn't want to still do it in ten years' time anyway. She thought it would probably be a much better decision to stay focused on her career and make great money that way, so that she could buy the house on the beach that she dreamed of owning.

When she wasn't working, she would be consuming huge amounts of learning from podcasts and books. She felt like she had so much to learn and was overwhelming herself by comparing where she was to other business gurus who had been in their areas of expertise for years! This then fed into making her feel even less qualified and less knowledgeable, increasing the worries and doubts that she could ever do this.

What was the point in wanting to have her own business as a consultant and have the freedom to travel and live life on her terms when she could never ever possibly be as good as these people already out there doing it?

This was a perfect example of how the mind works to keep you safe and leans on those beliefs you have running away in the background. Her limiting belief of *not being good enough* was showing up as not being *qualified* enough, fuelling her to want to become more qualified.

This trick that your mind plays beautifully is its *seek and destroy* function. It seeks out evidence to prove itself right and destroys evidence to the contrary, which contradicts the belief that it currently holds. The mind doesn't want you to see this alternative. It's perfectly happy with the one it has as it has been there all these years and it has safely and successfully got you this far.

---

"Your mind is always working to prove itself right."
*Donna & Cheryl*

---

Your job is to raise your awareness. It's your ongoing work to identify what your mind is doing and where it's working against what you truly desire, keeping you small and preventing you from becoming all you are destined to be. Then we can give it the evidence to support the outcome we want. We override the system.

We are going to start doing that right now. Your subconscious mind, which is where your beliefs are sitting, accepts whatever information you give to it and repetition is key to this reprogramming. This is where mantras or positive affirmations come into play.

## TIME TO KEEP IT REAL

Now you are going to create your new mantra (or you may call it a positive affirmation) of what it is you want to believe.

Think of the limiting beliefs you highlighted earlier and now you're effectively going to state the opposite.

So for example if your main negative affirmation is, 'I'm not qualified enough,' you can now start to positively affirm, 'I am an expert in my field,' or something that feels good to you.

It's important that it feels good when you say it and it states how you want to be once this mantra has done its job.

NEW MANTRA: I AM...

Save this in your phone, have it on a post-it where you sit. Repeat as many times per day as you can.

## CHAPTER SUMMARY

- Your life, your story, your life lessons have such power.
- Unprocessed life experiences are being carried around with us and are impacting our confidence and happiness today.
- Your subconscious mind is operating from the Belief System it currently has and you have to do the inner work to clear out the rubble.
- The mind always works to prove itself right so will look for evidence to support its current belief system.
- We all have limiting beliefs and our work is to keep finding, challenging and replacing them.

**My aha moment from this chapter is:**

# 5

# AM I A PSYCHO BITCH?

> *"It's not what you think you are that holds you back, it's what you think you're not."*
>
> — DENIS WAITLEY

**Donna**

Mr Bailey was one of my favourite teachers when I was in primary school. He was a great big bear of a man and I always remember him wearing one of those big brown furry Russian hats. He had a deep gravelly voice and the kindest brown eyes. I loved being in his class and I would soak up everything he taught us like a sponge. Then one day he told us that we would be having a test.

I remember that whoosh of blood up to my head and this feeling of panic rising through my body. "What if I'm no good at this 'test'?"

What would happen? Would I not be able to be in his class? Would my parents be angry? Would they be even worse than that... would they be *disappointed*?

I went home from school that day and cried, sobbed myself to sleep. Through the night I woke up and I knew I was going to be sick. I was so ill through the night that my Mam had to keep me off school the next day because she thought I had a stomach bug. But I knew it was the horror at the thought of this test and the fear of letting everyone down.

Let's press pause right here.

I have racked my brain about this over the years and I have no reason that I can recall to warrant such a strong reaction to being told there was a test. Sure, I had lost at a few dance competitions and, Lord knows, I never won any races on sports day but I had not 'failed' in any sense that I could recall.

## IMPOSTER SYNDROME

The reality was that I did really well in school – the teachers loved me because I was such a geek and always asked for extra homework! My parents always told me that as long as I did my best, everything was ok. I had no evidence to tell me anything other than that I would be ok in the test and if I wasn't - that was ok too. But my little mind just was not on that wavelength.

That right there is one of my earliest memories of Imposter Syndrome.

Imposter Syndrome is a cluster of various psychological symptoms that stem from believing that we aren't good enough and we are going to 'get found out'. When you have it, you feel like you got your results through luck, not through the talents that you have. You often look super confident and shiny on the outside but on the inside you are one hot mess of self-doubt and feel like you're a fraud who is faking their way through life.

High performing women are particularly impacted by it and if you check out Google, you'll find stats showing that as many as 80-90% of us are impacted by it. Crazy or what? Technically, the inference is that *you* are the Imposter because you don't feel good enough in situations, but we flip it and say that the syndrome is the Imposter because it isn't welcome and likes to gate-crash events.

> *"Even though I had sold 70 million albums, there I was feeling like, 'I'm not good at this'."*
>
> — JENNIFER LOPEZ

There are different ways that this Imposter can show up in your life.

**Perfectionism**

You're not comfortable with your work being just 'ok'. It has to be perfect, better than last time, the best they've ever seen and you're unhappy when it isn't! Which usually means that you're not happy with most of what you produce – or what others do for you – because the 'perfect' badge of approval doesn't come out all that often. Until you hand something in, you'll keep pulling it apart thinking that it could be better. This may spill over into how you feel about your appearance, your relationships and your life.

**Procrastination**

You become paralysed with thinking about how hard, how difficult this 'thing' is going to be to do. How many obstacles will be in the way that you're going to have to overcome to get it done. Then you're worrying that you're not qualified enough and you're doubting that you're the right woman for the job – you're just not capable enough! You become overwhelmed at all of the stuff that could go wrong with this project of yours and then you tell yourself that actually you just don't *have the time* to do it – you have so many other things that are way more important right now.

**Overworking**

Do you think that hard work is one of your core values? Do you feel driven to be 'first one in, last one out' when it comes to the working day? Do you get that internal high-five secretly when you feel like you've worked harder and longer than anyone else that week? And you're totally ok with other people taking breaks to eat and pee but for you, no way. That's lazy. You don't have time to take your lunch or take breaks because you feel guilty if you're not working. Unless you're driving yourself to a state of steady burnout, you feel like a slacker.

**Comparisonitis**

Everyone is doing it better than you. They all look like they totally know what they're doing. And they look better when they're doing it. They totally have their shit together, unlike you who are just winging it. Whether it's the other Mams at school who baked the brownies from scratch whereas you just ran into Tesco on the way to school to grab shop bought ones or the other business owners online who are visible and always looking gorgeous. When you turn up to a meeting you feel like everything that comes out of your mouth sounds stupid and you hate the sound of your own voice. Yep, everyone is just better than you at doing life.

### Inner Crazy Lady

She's the voice in your head that is relentless in telling you how you're going to fail, you're not qualified enough and that even when you do muster up the courage to speak, nobody actually wants to hear. She's your very own Mean Girl and she comes completely uninvited to the party and doesn't leave unless she's dragged out kicking and screaming and even then, she's at the back door banging to be in. She's brutal with her opinions, free flowing with her insults and never shy when it comes to telling you that you're going to fuck it up so why bother even giving it a go. The Buddhists may have called it 'Monkey Mind' but that image is way too cute for the bitch you're mentally wrestling with daily.

### Past and Future Tripping

It's already happened. "It's in the past" as Rafiki says in *The Lion King* but you *cannot... let... it... lie.* You ruminate over it. You lie awake in bed with the details going through your head over and over and over again. Each time you get a bit angrier, a bit more panicked, that you didn't do the right thing, that you could have done it better, that you didn't get it 'perfect' the first time. How could you not have known? Why didn't you do it differently? What the hell were you thinking? You're so stupid! You are never going to learn, you always fuck this stuff up, what the hell is wrong with you? The guilt is palpable, eating you up from the inside out.

Or maybe it hasn't even happened yet and you're already freaking out about how many ways it's going to go wrong. You're filled with worry about the fifty million scenarios that will lead to the thing not going to plan. Whether it's a holiday, job interview, date, kids' party or big meeting, your thoughts are consumed with the fear and dread of how badly it's all going to turn out and it will all be *your fault* because yet again, you let people down and couldn't quite get your shit together. It's all on you, lady. You're already feeling lashings of guilt in advance of the impending doom.

> *"When I won the Oscar, I thought it was a fluke. I thought everybody would find out, and they'd take it back. They'd come to my house, knocking on the door, 'Excuse me, we meant to give that to someone else. That was going to Meryl Streep.'"*
>
> — JODIE FOSTER

Imposter Syndrome *sucks.*

It's an exhausting daily mental bloody battle that you're fighting where there are rarely any winners. Even when you do have a 'small' success you can't languish in it for more than a nano-second because now you have to somehow manage to pull that rabbit out of the hat again to prove to yourself that it wasn't a fluke. Good luck with that.

All of the above symptoms of Imposter Syndrome are things that I have personally dealt with from being a kid in Mr Bailey's class and throwing up at the thought of a test to this day. The game changing moment for me, though, was when I learned that Imposter Syndrome was a *thing*. Up to that moment, I grew up thinking that the voice in my head was real. That I was actually a complete fake who didn't get any results and just held on to the coattails of the successes my teams had. I couldn't ever accept any praise for anything I did because I didn't think I deserved it.

Whether you knew before reading this that you too have Imposter Syndrome or whether reading this has brought a biblical-bolt-of-lightning-style revelation to you, we want you to hear this...

You are not crazy.

You are not a psycho bitch.

You are not a fake who is winging it and is about to get found out.

You have Imposter Syndrome and it can be managed. The volume can be turned down and you can change the pattern and start to believe that you *are* worthy, good enough, smart enough and lovable enough to live a happy and fulfilled life.

It's totally possible for you and trust me, I'm living proof that with work, retraining your Belief System and doing all the other stuff that Cheryl and I are showing you in this book, you can tell your Inner Crazy Lady to go take a long walk off a short bridge.

---

"You're not a psycho bitch - you just have Imposter Syndrome."
*Donna & Cheryl*

---

**ESTELLE**

I gave my Imposter a name, a personality and she became Estelle because she reminded me of Joey's agent from the TV show *Friends*. Now I know that Estelle is actually trying to keep me safe and wants me to be ok. I've made good friends with her and she doesn't get to push me around any more.

Mastering your mindset, learning how to create the thoughts that empower you and break free from the limiting beliefs that may have been running the show up until now is a challenge that we know that you're ready for. Otherwise, you wouldn't *still be reading this book*.

Knowing how to think better, to harness the power of your mind to bring about an inner environment that is loving, nurturing and also fun to be in, will change your life beyond measure. Learning how to live inside out, so that what you think and feel can then be physically manifested – in your relationships, career, money, purpose for being here – all starts with you knowing how to be the maestro of the thoughts that you think.

---

### TIME TO KEEP IT REAL

Time now to go and explore how your Imposter Syndrome is showing up in your life, how it's keeping you small and what your next steps are.

Head over to your Book Resources at www.therealyoumethod.com/book-resources

---

## MASKS

You may or may not be familiar with this term but let us tell you what it means to us. When you're going through your day-to-day life, in order not to look totally insane with some (or let's face it, on a bad day, all) of the unhelpful thoughts from your limiting beliefs racing through your head like rally cars on a racetrack going round and round and never seeming to get anywhere, you adopt your mask.

It's the face you put on so that you show up in a way that doesn't cause anyone to be concerned. You look just as the world expects you to – smiling, happy with all of your shit together. In 100% people pleasing mode, keeping all the crazy on the quiet. Locked down, real tight. It's your protective shell, it makes you feel safe, it helps you to feel like the you the world expects.

That's to say… the you that you *believe* that the world expects.

Not *The Real You*. Fuck, no. They can't handle that, right? Actually, let's face it, your Imposter has you believing that they would probably hate you if they knew what you were really like. You've got away all this time with kidding them that you're this great person so you just keep applying the makeup and heading out into the world fully armoured with your smile, humour and your self-deprecating one-liners.

> *"It's not fear that gets in the way of showing up - it's armor. It's the behaviours we use to self-protect. We can be afraid and brave at the same time. But the armor suffocates courage and cages our hearts."*
>
> — BRENÉ BROWN

When we met Yvette she was sitting in a meeting room at the UK HQ of the company she worked at – basically, it was a glass box. It was early morning and she was equipped with her obligatory morning coffee to get her going, dressed in her white shirt and navy suit jacket. Her hair was suitably tamed into a ponytail with pins to keep it falling in her gorgeous face. She was evidently very nervous speaking to us and was very keen for us to know she was really very happy and grateful for her life.

The one thing that wasn't quite where it needed to be was her health. She felt like it was out of balance and whilst she was a qualified Kundalini teacher, she wasn't being consistent with her practice, food or balance of personal and work time.

Now, we want you to know that Yvette completely bought into this at that time. She herself was completely convinced in her conscious mind that her health was the reason she had been guided to us through a mutual friend.

But what we know is that *the thing is never the thing.*

## THE THING IS NEVER THE THING

You see, our mind can play all kinds of tricks on us. The use of masks is a great example. When you do something day in, day out, it becomes second nature. It kind of fuses with who you believe you are and you form this as a habit. You accept it. You come to believe that it's who you truly are.

But of course, this *isn't* really you. It's not who you were born to be. This is the False Self hiding in plain sight. It's the personality our Ego has created over the years. The Ego or False Self is our self-image and it's attached to a certain identity, a particular set of labels. It has an overinflated sense of importance and a need to demonstrate its power through the things we have or the things we do. It can get in the way of you getting to know *The Real You* - who is *way* more than your body, your job title or how much you have in the bank.

Before you become aware of this, in your mind the you in the mask is real. Anyone looking at you would never know the difference. On the inside, well, that's a different story altogether. It feels like warfare because you know this doesn't feel good and you feel out of kilter in some way.

For Yvette, her False Self was showing up as this corporate woman in a lovely suit, in a glass office with a very important job. But she knew that something was off and just wasn't clicking. She looked fairly *lost* sitting there in that glass box.

> *"Ego is simply an idea of who you are that you carry around with you."*
>
> — DR. WAYNE DYER

*Lost* is the word that comes up most often from our new clients. You forgot who you really are. It feels like something is missing from your life, there's something not quite right but you can't seem to put your finger on it. You find yourself reading books, listening to podcasts, seeking that missing piece of the puzzle that's going to make you feel like you again. But you're not quite sure what it is or where you left it.

For Yvette, sitting in her corporate suit in her glass box, she knew there was something holding her back and how she felt about her body seemed like the obvious answer. Especially given that in her mid-thirties, she had undergone a radical hysterectomy due to cervical cancer. She was still coming to terms with her relationship with her body in many ways.

But there was more to it than that.

She knew she was having difficulty getting over her views and true opinions at work. She felt like she couldn't quite be herself, but she didn't know why because she described herself as an outgoing and confident person who had plenty of opinions to share, so she was confused at herself. It didn't add up. The pieces weren't all fitting together. Somehow her voice was being lost and she just couldn't work out why, leading her to feel frustrated, angry at herself and her Imposter Syndrome was full on.

As our session with her was now warmed up, we could see how much her energy had shifted. The well-practised smile and the self-deprecating jokes had stopped and she had become tuned in to the awareness of the thing that was missing that she couldn't put her finger on. The mask was starting to lose its grip and was slowly sliding to the floor. She was still mindful of how grateful she was, particularly given that she was in remission from cancer, but the guilt she was carrying was preventing her from being able to say what she *really wanted to have happen*.

So we asked her, "If in twelve months' time nothing has changed in your life, how will you feel?"

*The mask was off.*

Now purely in the emotion of feeling into that question, there was no more pretence of trying to keep that brave face on, the one that the rest of the world saw every day. The thought of spending another year of her life in a glass box was too much to take; the thought alone was suffocating to her.

She gathered herself together, scrambling to make sense of her thoughts and these new emotions as she told us, "I can't live another year like this. I have this awful fear of dying with a song inside me left unsung."

There it was: the admission out loud that she wanted *more* from her life. She had no idea what, but she recognised in that moment that she had been playing it safe and she knew that underneath all of the second guessing that she was good enough... that she was capable of more.

## WANTING MORE

These conversations are huge breakthrough moments for a client. Or indeed anyone. Getting real with yourself and saying out loud that you want more makes it so much more real. That makes it scary! With that admission, the next step is to get accountable and take action. There are a few big reasons why we often don't go that far when something pops up in our head and we swat it down like an annoying fly. Thwack! The reasons are as follows:

### 1. Greed

When we admit we want more, then we believe that we are saying that what we have isn't enough. We feel that we are being ungrateful for what we have. That doesn't sit well with us. It's greedy. We are raised to be grateful for what we have, trained from a young age not to complain because there are always people worse off than ourselves. Whether it's the food on our plate, the roof over our head or the job that we have – be grateful for it! Someone would love to have what you have!

And it's true, someone would. But that does *not* mean that you don't get to want more from your life because it is *your life*. It doesn't for a heartbeat mean that you don't feel love and appreciation for the things you have right now. For Yvette, having a great job, surviving cancer, having an incredible hubby and spending her free time travelling to see her fave heavy rock bands was a blessed existence.

> *"I want to make women laugh. I want to make them feel beautiful in their own skin. I want to empower them to use their voice and not apologize. And I want a jet."*
>
> — AMY SCHUMER

When we are told to count our blessings as kids, it seems to create the belief that your blessings are a finite number. If you get to one hundred you've used them all up and that's your lot. Don't be greedy and ask for more. You've had yours. But it's so not true – it's the opposite! Blessings are in abundance for all of us; they're never-ending.

**2. Fear**

Fundamentally, we are walking around not liking ourselves. We are listening all day long to that Imposter in our head, our inner Mean Girl telling us that we are all of the things on the previous pages. She's a bitch! She has nothing nice to say but we have been tuned in to her for so long we believe the crap she's saying. We actually believe those things about ourselves so why would we want to find out even more about ourselves? We don't like the stuff we already know so we can't imagine there's going to be any good stuff in there.

We are afraid to get to know ourselves. We have kind of come to terms with the version of us who wears the mask. The people on the outside seem to quite like the person we present to the world so we are hanging on in there. We don't want to lose that because most days we aren't quite sure how it's happening – so best not rock the boat.

> *"The fears we don't face become our limits."*
>
> — ROBIN SHARMA

Quite frankly, we are scared of what we might actually find if we start to ask ourselves some of those big questions. Such as, "Am I happy?" Nope, best avoid them altogether. Who knows what we could unearth? Swat that fly hard and fast – no room for that buzzing around in our head. It simply doesn't occur to us that we will find untold jewels, that we will connect with powers inside us that make us feel unstoppable. We are terrified of liking ourselves even less and not knowing what to do next. Whilst Yvette didn't like that glass box, *she was safe there...* it was what she knew.

**3. Success**

This may seem the most bizarre one of all but you would be shocked if we told you how many of our clients are terrified at first of being successful, of having it all. I mean who really gets to have it all anyway? Surely that's an urban myth... how can that even be possible? The vast majority of us don't believe that 'all' exists.

When we are on the cusp of having it all, when we are about to leap off and finally get everything we dreamed of having, our finger comes out and we press that big red button that says STOP! We make sure something goes wrong so that we hit the brakes and with our subconscious in safety mode we create the problem, blocker or obstacle so that we know where the problem lies and we can rest easy again.

How many times have you sabotaged a relationship that was going so well it was unnerving for you so you created an argument or decided that something must be wrong with him so you start to check his phone? Or what about your diet - you're powering along, feeling great, almost at your goal then it's all too much and you press the self-destruct button and eat cheese like they're closing the French borders.

In his brilliant book *The Big Leap* Gay Hendricks beautifully terms this condition the 'Upper Limit Problem'. Gay describes how each of us has our own bandwidth for feeling good. When we max out that bandwidth, we create or find a problem to bring ourselves back into the feel-good range that is comfortable for us.

## HAVING IT ALL

It may be ok for rich people or movie stars who look fabulous to 'have it all' but for us that just doesn't seem attainable. As Yvette sat in her glass box with her hair all neat and her corporate armour on, it didn't seem remotely possible to her that she could have her own marketing agency. No part of her mind considered it an option because her mind and her False Self found the story of her being a contractor and wanting to get a permanent job and a promotion so much more reasonable and feasible than flights of fancy about owning her own company.

> *"Our deepest fear is not that we are inadequate. Our deepest fear is that we are powerful beyond measure."*
>
> — MARIANNE WILLIAMSON

But here's the thing.

Once you hold a mirror up and ask your False Self, "Is that true?" there's sometimes a pause. And in that pause, there lies *infinite possibility. The Real You* is a being of boundless creative potential and power who is plugged into The Universe itself where all things are available.

A year after our initial chat with Yvette, she set up her own business, dyed her hair pink and matched her corporate income in her first month in business wearing a Motorhead t-shirt with her tattoos on display. This spiritual, badass, marketing maverick no longer sits in a glass box. She smashed it up and vows never to set foot in it again.

---

"Imposter Syndrome isn't keeping you stuck...
You knowing how to manage it is."
*Donna & Cheryl*

---

Now she looks back and realises that she was so far out of alignment from her True Self, worlds away from how she feels today. But at the time she didn't have this insight; she didn't recognise that she was trapped in the glass box. Yvette wasn't consciously aware that she was trapped and not living out her purpose. It didn't even cross her mind.

Today she dives out of bed with so much love, appreciation and happiness as she has found fulfilment. Her soul is nourished on a daily basis whilst being true to herself. Without the masks or the pretence. How amazeballs is that?

Imagine living your life every day without the masks, or the people pleasing, the saying yes when you really mean no. Without that funny feeling in your tummy that something just doesn't feel quite right. Feeling guilty that you want more. Thinking, is this really 'it'?

Now Is Your Time to give yourself permission to want *more*. To have it all. To live the largest, richest expression of your life humanly possible. Nothing you want is off the table. If you want it, then it's already available to you.

The Universe is waiting to help you create the life of your dreams and all you have to do right now is start imagining what 'having it all' looks like for you. You don't need to want to have pink hair or tattoos or want to blow off your corporate career or wear a Motorhead t-shirt every day. You just have to lean into the desire that there might be something more.

In Yvette's moment of awakening, she realised it was more important to live a life full of happiness and authenticity than to die with a song inside her unsung... and look where this took her.

Your journey begins when you say, "Yes!"

Yes to yourself. Yes to the decision that you are worthy of having it all – abundance, prosperity, health, love... whatever your heart desires.

It doesn't cost you anything to say YES right now, here, in this moment and to exploring what having it all looks like for you.

---

## TIME TO KEEP IT REAL

So are you in?

What did Yvette's story bring up for you?

How will you feel if you're where you are now in a year?

Which of the three reasons we listed are holding you back?

Journal for twenty minutes without stopping on what 'having it all' would look like for you.

---

**CHAPTER SUMMARY**

- Imposter Syndrome shows up in different ways and is the feeling that you're a fraud, not responsible for your success and is the voice in your head telling you that you're not good enough.
- You're not a psycho bitch – you just have an Inner Crazy Lady who has been running the show for some time and her days are now numbered.
- Your False Self / Ego is you with all of the armour and masks on but it's not *The Real You*. *The Real You* is so much more than any of the labels you've attached to yourself up until now and is completely limitless.
- It's ok to want more and The Universe is ready to give it to you.
- The reasons we have given ourselves to not follow our dreams seem real, but they're not.
- Start saying YES to pursuing your heart's desires and the biggest vision for your life and work out what having it all would look like for you.

**My aha moment from this chapter is:**

6

## MAKE YOUR DESIRES GREATER THAN YOUR FEAR

> *"There is nothing that belief plus a burning desire cannot make real."*
>
> — NAPOLEON HILL

How often do you hear yourself saying, "I don't know," when you're asked what you want? Think about it, even when you go to a restaurant and you're ordering food... how often do you start talking about what you *don't* want to eat first?

"What do you fancy for lunch?"

"I don't fancy pasta; it's too heavy. I'm not eating dairy right now, so nothing with dairy."

"Great – what do you fancy for lunch?"

Or when it comes to looking for a new relationship. When you're asked what you want from your new guy...

"I definitely don't want another guy who spends every Saturday watching football. And I don't want him to be needy and messaging me all the time. Oh, and I don't want a guy who is in the gym all the time."

Maybe you're looking for a new job. What are you looking for in your next role?

"I don't want a company who doesn't value my opinion. I also don't want to work for a boss who emails me at all hours of the day and night. Or who micromanages me."

Get the picture?

## TIME TO GET CLEAR

We spend a lot of time and energy talking about all the things that we *don't* want. It's usually our default when we are asked about what we *do* want. We are super clear on what we don't want to have happen, what we don't want to eat, who we don't want to meet, where we don't want to work.

There are always two sides to the coin – what we want and what we don't want. Our programming generally is strongly in favour of focusing on the thing that we don't want. Our focus is magnetically drawn to listing out everything that would not bring us happiness or satisfaction. It's actually less natural to us or easy for us to talk about the thing that we *do* want. We spend far less time in daily thought or conversation focusing on the things we would love to have happen.

When was the last time you sat and just daydreamed about how you would love your life to be? How often do you give yourself permission and carve out space to start getting super conscious about what you want to manifest in your life? We are betting the answer is either, "Never" or, "Not for ages!"

That's usually because:

- You're really busy and you don't have time.
- There's no point fantasising, it's not reality.
- You've made your bed so you've no choice but to lie in it.
- You've got responsibilities so sitting dwelling on pipedreams is a luxury you can't afford.
- Things like that don't happen to you, get real.

Which reason one is yours? Or maybe it's all of them?

Daydreaming is something that we do naturally as kids but as we grow up, the adulting really gets in the way. When your mind does wander off to future moments in time, let's be frank – you're usually future-tripping and NOT in a good way. As your mind wanders, the thoughts are usually centred around stuff going wrong. You imagine all the stuff you don't want to happen, coming true.

It happens every day. How many of these have you future-tripped about...

- You finally get that new job you've always wanted then start panicking that you won't perform well.
- You know you have to be up early for a meeting so you obsess about not sleeping in (then have a crappy sleep looking at the clock every hour).
- Your three-year-old has a tantrum and you picture them being a teenage delinquent and everyone knows it was your shitty parenting skills.

- You finally meet the guy of your dreams then wonder what is actually wrong with him.
- You hit your goal weight and then immediately stress that you probably won't be able to maintain it.
- You have a beautiful family occasion then feel sad that someday soon it will all change.
- You set up your brand new business then worry you'll fail, look stupid and lose everything.

What else would you add to the list? Observe how many times a day you do this – it will blow your mind!

---

"What you focus on you create more of."
*Donna & Cheryl*

---

## IMAGINATION

Your imagination is vast; it's totally without limits. It can come up with scenarios beyond your wildest dreams. Sadly, the ones we conjure up are usually all negative. Now we want you to flip it. We want it to land on the other side of the coin. What if every single 'what if' you had, ended up with you getting exactly what *you do want*? If every single 'what if' future scenario resulted in the best possible outcome? Imagine that every time you flipped that coin, the 'what if' is the perfect upshot?

What would that look like and more importantly, how would that *feel* to be thinking in that way every day instead of always mentally picturing the worst?

Imagine that this is how you think...

- You're excited for your interview and can see how well you're going to show up.
- You hit your weight goal and you know that you now have this nailed.
- You meet the man of your dreams and you picture your happy-ever-after knowing you finally have met the man you deserve.
- You launch your new business and picture all of the clients you're going to serve and how you're going to celebrate your success in years to come.
- You buy your new home and you picture family Christmases and seeing everyone happy and full of joy.
- You decide to have a family and imagine doing fun things together and making memories through the years.
- Your three-year-old throws a tantrum and you picture in your mind telling them this funny story when they're older.

You get the picture.

You may not have realised up until this moment that you even do that. It's just your 'normal' – you and most other people! But what if you chose differently when it comes to your thoughts? What if you were in the driving seat of your thoughts and feelings, not just some passenger, white-knuckling the ride and hoping for the best?

Start using this power at your fingertips to create your dreams into existence.

## DESIRES

What we know is that our lives got exponentially better when we started to get more aware, more conscious of the beliefs we have, the thoughts we were thinking and then focusing on what we wanted more than what we didn't want.

That clarity on what it is that you want is priceless. It's also one of the questions that when we ask it of our clients, elicits a very strong, emotional response, because we go through our lives failing to consciously acknowledge these desires that exist within us. They sit there unexpressed, suppressed, waiting for the day that someone comes and asks them to show themselves.

For too many people, that day never comes.

They go to the grave filled with unspoken and unacknowledged desires.

*We don't want for that to be you.*

We want you to know, trust and live out your desires, because honestly, if they weren't meant for you to have manifested then you wouldn't have them in the first place. This is The Universe in action! Those desires you have are those nudges from The Universe, wanting you to expand and have those things in your life. So don't question whether you *should* have them. Imagine that it's actually already yours!

---

"Just ask.
The Universe is waiting to give it to you."
*Donna & Cheryl*

---

This is one of our favourite things to do with our clients. Giving them permission to go and spend time dreaming of the things they want to manifest into their lives. Some write a list; others do a vision board or sit with a partner and go wild mapping out both individual and couple desires.

Some of the things we have seen on these lists and then have witnessed come into reality are...

- Cars
- A speedboat
- Dream homes
- Weight and health goals
- Relocating
- Land
- Becoming an author
- New businesses
- Financial windfalls
- Promotions
- New careers
- £10k months
- £100k months
- Becoming a millionaire
- New partners
- Babies
- Business expansion
- Global contracts with brands
- Work and life balance
- Pay rises
- Holiday homes
- Puppies
- A business partner
- Holidays

It is so much fun to watch clients start to dream up the things they want to show up in their lives and then when the real magic starts to happen and these things begin to appear – well, that's when our belief in what we can achieve really starts to shift up a gear.

---

## TIME TO KEEP IT REAL

It's your turn. Now you have permission to do your Desires List!

We want you to answer this question: What do I want?

Stop now, grab a cup of coffee (wine is obviously ok too if that's how you see it happening!) and start this journey of uncovering exactly *what you want.*

Head over to your Desires List in your Book Resources at www.therealyoumethod.com/book-resources

Sit for twenty minutes and write without stopping.

Note down as many things as you can think of, flood the pages with your desires! It doesn't matter how big, how small, how far out – list each and every one of them without filtering.

This is your personal Desires List and it's for your eyes only so go for it.

Read this every single day and get excited about the things on it!

---

## THE F WORD

But look, before we break open the goals box, we have to go somewhere with you first. We have to talk about the good old F word again. It's impossible to have this conversation without first addressing why you didn't already have this list of Desires you've just written out. And that F word (on this occasion) is FEAR.

In the last chapter we talked to you about Fear and how it can stop you getting to know who you truly are. Our Fear pops up constantly in our lives; it disguises itself so cleverly too. Much of the time when it's in control, what is actually happening in your head will seem totally normal. You'll often find yourself with incredibly valid reasons for not being able to do something. They're so 'normal' and 'realistic' that you won't even stop to question them. They make total sense to your conscious mind, therefore you just accept them as fact and continue to move through your day.

You won't be aware that in actual fact it's your Fear doing the talking, driving the decisions and therefore in control of your life.

Don't believe us? Well, here are a couple of stories to show you how insidious this Fear of yours can be. It's super smart, alarmingly cunning and highly plausible.

### Cheryl

I used to say to Donna that I would have a business 'one day' when I had £50k in the bank. I said that if I ever started a business, I would need the money to pay my bills for a whole year before I would entertain the idea of starting a business. *Yet I never started this savings pot.* I didn't put any money aside – not one single penny – towards what I professed to be this big goal of mine to have my own coaching business. I used to say it would be in my mid-forties. Then as I got into my forties I said it would be when I retired. It just kept moving further out and the magical pot of money that would enable this dream to happen didn't ever take shape.

So if the money was the thing stopping me, then why wasn't I saving for the goal? I earned a great salary, my husband, Graham, and I were comfortable and saved or paid for other goals in life – so why not this?

Simple.

*Fear.*

I was scared of failing. What if I went for it and it all went wrong? Where would my security be? That's where the money to pay the bills for a year came in. That was my back-up plan. For when I failed at being a Coach.

> *"There is only one thing that makes a dream impossible to achieve: the fear of failure. When you want something, all the universe conspires in helping you achieve it."*
>
> — PAULO COELHO

## DAYDREAM BELIEVER

One of our clients, Joanne, has a brilliant entrepreneurial brain. She comes up with new ideas for businesses all of the time. When we first met her, she was already successfully leading several businesses and what first came across as being pretty humble about her accomplishments, we soon realised was way more than that – she was actively hiding them.

She was so uncomfortable celebrating her ideas, achievements and dreams that she shied away from engaging in conversations about them with friends and family. When we sat and chatted with her you could see how they were literally flowing out of her. She was like a bottle of champagne that had popped its cork and the fizzing bubbles were flowing everywhere!

When we delved into why she felt so unable to share this side of herself with her loved ones, at first she said that they wouldn't be interested, that they would likely be bored listening to her. What we know from these conversations is that what first presents as the reason why someone is in avoidance behaviour, usually isn't the reason. It's just the reason they're conscious of at that point. Remember, the thing is never the thing, so we kept going…

"Who am I to be talking about all these big ideas to everyone?"

There it was: the kind of judgement that we know is an internal judgement being reflected back out onto the world. What was really going on was that this bright, beautiful entrepreneur, Mam to four boys and loving wife clearly felt that she wasn't good enough to be talking about these things. Her fear of not being good enough and worrying that other people would also think that, was what was keeping her cork well and truly stuck in her bottle.

Her ambitions of running multiple profitable businesses, having luxurious holidays with all of her family, owning a huge home... were all bottled up inside of her because she thought that other people would laugh at her. She even worried that they would dislike her for it, that her friends wouldn't want to know her. The valid reason to her conscious mind for not sharing was simply that everyone would be bored. It wasn't until we peeled back the layers that she could see how this Fear had cleverly clothed itself and was keeping her stuck in a pattern of being successful but with a very firm lid on how far that would go.

Your Fear is such a clever master manipulator; it has you dancing to a tune and you don't even know there's music playing!

> *"There is no illusion greater than fear."*
>
> — LAO TZU

The thing it's important for you to know right now is that we aren't aware that these Fears exist or that they're the ones in the driving seat. We have no clue! This is why they're so damn clever, and if left unchallenged will have you sailing along in life for years being 'ok' and 'fine' but keeping you from doing big, scary arse stuff because your Fear is designed to keep you safe.

Its intention is really positive. *Your Fear is trying to keep you safe.*

It manifests as your day-to-day thinking and reasoning as to why you can't have the things that deep down you would love to have sometimes. It's not real! It's just an illusion. Becoming aware of this Fear, of what it's telling you, of what it's keeping you from and how it's keeping you stuck is nothing short of miraculous. It gives you the opportunity to see your choices, your options and your potential with totally new eyes.

## TIME TO KEEP IT REAL

So what's this all for? Why get conscious about this Fear at all…

We all have Fear: it's part of our human makeup but deciding whether or not you tune in to that as your primary source for decision making is a choice that we all have control over once we are aware that it is happening. Take ten minutes and journal on these questions.

What is it you're holding Fear about?

What is it getting in the way of you doing and being?

Who would you be if this wasn't stopping you?

Allow your Fear to have less power over you and remember, you're in the Director's Chair of your own movie!

## BIG HAIRY GOALS

Ok, this section is going to sting a bit, especially if you're from a corporate background. If you haven't thought we were crazy up until now, this may well be the point where you decide otherwise! Our job as your Coaches isn't for you to like us, remember. Our job is to help you have insight that you didn't have before. It's to help you see your own potential as we see it – totally limitless! It's for you to have a different perspective on your life that you didn't have up until now. Sometimes that can be uncomfortable for us. We like everything to be mapped out and all neat.

Here's the thing...

When we are in a normal work environment, we want to know what we are going after and then there will be a twenty-page project plan and owners for every single action, process and outcome right up until it is delivered.

We fixate on *how* our goal is going to be achieved. We dissect each element of the plan to make sure that we haven't missed out any information, that we haven't overlooked any potential risks and that we have mitigated against all possible threats to our success. This thorough approach and having super SMART objectives (Specific, Measurable, Actionable, Realistic, Time Bound) in our jobs make us feel like we have it all under control and help us to look like the experts in our field.

For most businesses it is absolutely essential to have this level of rigour around objectives, goals and project pathways.

Except this isn't a work project. This is *your life* we are encouraging you to get real about here. In real life when we approach our goals this way, there are a few issues:

1. When you don't know how to get there, you don't even start. You think of something you would love and then your thoughts quickly shift to the practicalities of it all and before you know it, you've put it back in that box. We feel compelled to know what each and every step is from where we are now to having the goal landed.
2. We get hung up on the plan and lose perspective of why we actually wanted to do it in the first place. It can drain our energy very quickly being in the weeds of the baby

steps rather than remaining connected to the bigger vision of what this end goal will mean for your life. That makes it much easier for us to start questioning ourselves and whether we are on the right path in the first place because we have become disconnected from our BIG goal.

3. If something happens along the way that is 'off plan' we perceive it as 'going wrong' when actually it could be working to our benefit. We deem that it must be bad because it's not the way we planned it, so then we think we are failing and sometimes then start coming up with a new plan altogether! As Gabby Bernstein says in *The Universe Has Your Back*, Obstacles are a Detour in The Right Direction.
4. When we are fixed on one course of action and another opportunity appears, we ignore it as it's 'not in the plan'. We have a habit of thinking that our way, our original way and our plan is THE plan and exclude automatically that there could be a better, easier or more fun way of doing things. A bit like a horse wearing blinkers, we see only the actions that are laid out in front of us and fail to see all of the other opportunities available to us at all times. The Universe has way more resources at its disposal than we do.
5. Having all of the detail nailed and you focusing on that rather than how amazing it will be when you have the thing you want, is way less fun. It doesn't *feel* anywhere near as good. Looking at a project plan for your goal is nowhere near as much fun as daydreaming and imagining how utterly incredible you're going to feel when you have achieved this bewitching BIG goal.

> *"You don't have to see the whole staircase, just take the first step."*
>
> — MARTIN LUTHER KING JR.

In short, you don't have to know how you're going to achieve your goal, you just have to know that you want it and believe it's possible for you. We actually want for you not to know because if you already know, the goal probably isn't big enough! So for now just have the goal and release any expectations of knowing how you're going to make it happen.

## YOU ALWAYS HAVE A GOAL

Your goals in life aren't meant to drain you and add more stress to your life. They're meant to be exciting, fill you with joy, and bring you a huge amount of fun and anticipation. Are yours doing that for you right now? And to be clear, we all have goals. Every one of us is getting up every single day of our lives and working towards a goal. Whether your goal is to:

- Just get through the week
- Not gain any weight
- Binge watch the latest Netflix series
- Not lose your temper with that guy at work
- Have an ok or fine day
- Not let tech get the better of you
- Not look for your dream job
- Stay unhappy in your marriage
- Keep pleasing people and never say 'No'
- Stay small
- Stay in the rat race

- Keeping going at the job that sucks the life out of you

These things are all still goals because you're getting up every day and working towards making them happen. But they for sure aren't the goals that *set your soul on fire*. Yet these are the goals that most people wake up every day and strive for. Doesn't that boggle your mind? We are working ourselves like crazy just to get through life! Hitting burn out, living with constant levels of stress in our body doing all kinds of damage and the main goal is to get through to the weekend. Then we get two days off, eat and drink more – then rinse and repeat.

Too often we see people getting conscious about their life because something awful has happened. Someone dies, you get sick, you lose your business – there's some kind of wakeup call that shakes you to your core and you ask yourself then, "What is really important to me?" This is exactly what happened to us too when Davie died. We want you to have that same wakeup call *without* the major life event.

Have your moment of awakening right now.

You don't need to have the pain of loss or trauma to create a new shift in your life. And if you're reading this right now because that is exactly what has happened for you – then that's ok too. Let's use that energy to get behind generating a magical shift in your life.

## SOUL GOALS

Creating a vision of how you want your life to be isn't just for rich people, spiritual people or someone that you've marked somehow 'special'. It's your birthright to experience joy, love, and abundance in whatever way speaks to you. And no, that doesn't mean that you get a free pass on any of the more testing stuff, but we just need to learn that the ups and downs are part of life.

Nobody is immune to those events and moments. It's part of the journey for everyone. The people who you think are rocking life, who have these big goals, who are making an impact and seeing big things land in their lives are also dealing with the same crap as you are. Don't get sucked into thinking that they had it easier, got lucky or had some sort of golden pathway paved ready for them.

Whatever they can do, so can you. Your starting points may be different, that's all. It's still available to you.

You have your Desires List now; you have written out the things that you want to welcome into your life. Go look at that list now and ask yourself, what is the one thing above all else that when you have reached it, will change the game for you?

This is what we love to call your 'Soul Goal'.

---

"You are the Writer, Director and Star of your own movie."
*Donna & Cheryl*

---

Your Soul Goal is the thing that until now you may have called a pipe dream. It's that thing that when you see other people have it or do it you think how amazing it is for them, without actually feeling like it's possible for you. When you think about how it would feel achieving this thing, you feel so overwhelmed with excitement, happiness and wonder, whilst at the same time maybe feeling like you could be sick! Sick with fear, nerves and even worry because you don't actually want to let yourself dare think what it would be like in case it doesn't come true. You're scared it won't happen so you have never allowed yourself to think of it.

We want you to do the opposite.

We want you to get under the skin of what that thing would feel like in your life. Open yourself up to the emotions this would bring up for you. Imagine in detail how your life would be.

> *"Nothing is as important as passion. No matter what you want to do with your life, be passionate."*
>
> — JON BON JOVI

Your Soul Goal will stir your emotions, create a strong physical reaction within you, awakening you to the potential of how life can really feel for you every single day of your time here. Having this kind of focus and vision in your life of something you're working towards that you're more than passionate about, you feel compelled towards, moved by, connected with, is the key to harnessing the rocket fuel to propel you forward.

When you rely only on motivation, it will ebb and flow. The energy you generate from having this internal soul fuel of being aligned to this vision of your life will support you in taking all the inspired action needed to get there. Wherever 'there' is for you and your Soul Goal.

---

"You don't have a motivation issue - you have a goal issue."
*Donna & Cheryl*

---

We can tell you right here and now that since we connected to our Soul Goal of coaching women all over the world to become the best version of themselves and to live their lives as their true, authentic selves with no need for masks... we haven't once had to rely on motivation to get us through the day. We haven't once wished for the weekend.

Let's get real and get you clear on what your Soul Goal is.

---

**TIME TO KEEP IT REAL**

Head over to your Book Resources at www.therealyoumethod.com/book-resources and work through the questions.

Then come back here and write below your own, personal, unique and inspiring Soul Goal.

My Soul Goal is:

---

## CHAPTER SUMMARY

- Get clear on what you do want instead of what you don't want.
- Spend time daydreaming and let your imagination go wild on all the great things you would love to have happen in your life.
- Your desires are there because The Universe wants you to give you those things.
- Read your Desires List every single day and imagine having those things.
- Fear is a normal human emotion but it's a decision to let it get in the way of your dreams.
- Set Big Hairy Goals that you have no idea how you will achieve.
- Your Soul Goal removes the need for motivation because it aligns you with your purpose.

**My aha moment from this chapter is:**

# 7

# REMEMBER HER?

> *"That's the real trouble with the world, too many people grow up."*
>
> — WALT DISNEY

**Donna**

When I was a little girl I used to put on my Mam's dressing gown and I had these little plastic shoes with a heel on... oh my God, I was so grown up... and I would run around the living room, dressing gown swirling behind me as I ran around and around imagining myself running down a spiral staircase because in my head, I was the wicked Queen from Snow White. Don't ask me why I didn't want to be Snow White, I have no idea, but I do remember believing that the Queen was way more interesting and pretty. I liked her crown – oh yes, I had a plastic tiara on my head too. You have to be dressed up the full part, right?

I could play like that for hours. I was an only child until I was seven so I had to get good at entertaining myself and I know I was never bored. My imagination knew no bounds. I could spend hours daydreaming and I loved writing stories and reading books. I loved animals and until I was well into my later teens, I really thought I was going to be the next David Attenborough and quite fancied the idea of travelling the world and stroking mountain gorillas and giant tortoises in the Galapagos Islands.

There was no part of my brain that said, "You can't be the wicked Queen, she's way prettier than you and far better at casting spells," or, "You'll never be smart enough to be a globally renowned biologist!"

## ANYTHING IS POSSIBLE

In my young mind, it was a done deal. Along with hundreds of other fantasies and dreams – which included being married to Christopher Reeve, being best friends with Sylvester Stallone, having a mansion like the one in Dynasty, having a rottweiler called Mandy, and having a super high-powered job where I got to have big hair and huge shoulder pads just like in L.A. Law.

When you're a kid, anything seems possible. We are constantly engaging the use of one of our biggest gifts and highest faculties – the gift of imagination.

Do you remember that feeling?

When absolutely anything was possible for you. Life was going to be this fabulous big adventure and you felt completely limitless. You would get gigantic butterflies thinking about how exciting it was going to be.

There was no filter.

None of this... "Oh well, there's already somebody else doing that so maybe not..."

There was only imagining it, seeing it, feeling it and *believing it was going to happen.*

It was SO much fun. And it didn't cost a penny!

You didn't sit and think, "Well, it might not happen so no point spending time thinking of that, what a waste!"

Nope. When we are young, we are Oscar winning actors, playing out the scenarios that run through our head, constantly being inspired by books, films and games. There's always a new idea, a new game to act out or a new story in our head. Sometimes we may not remember it as clearly but we all had this power to dream these huge, crazy, colourful dreams. And more importantly, we still do.

As we start adulting for a living, we forget who we wanted to be and we create the grown up version of ourselves. Usually way less fun, and filled with all of the limiting bullshit we talked about in the last chapter.

We start to think that it's silly, stupid, pointless, childish, unnecessary, not 'real life' and generally a waste of our super precious time.

But she's still in there, that little girl who could dream big and believed that anything was possible. Reconnect with her because you know what, she was on to something. You come into this world a total blank canvas, thinking BIG and with zero cap on *how* big you can go. Along your way, you start to doubt yourself, you start to listen to the opinions of others and you start to get smaller.

> *"The true sign of intelligence is not knowledge but imagination."*
>
> — ALBERT EINSTEIN

**Cheryl**

Going into 'Big School' when I was eleven, I was still playing with dolls, blissfully unaware of what other people thought of me, happily sailing through life in my own happy bubble. When I rocked up to Big School on day one, I had on white socks pulled up all the way, brown sandals on my larger than average feet and my large mop of black curls doing their own thing on my head.

As I stood in the gigantic school yard waiting for the bell to ring on the first day, I felt so small and lost. I didn't know many people starting at that school, so I was looking around the sea of faces, searching for a familiar one. It felt like a far cry from the small circle of close friends I had had up to this point, the ones I would run around the fields with behind our house. Laughing, confident and not a care in the world. Standing here now, I felt like a small fish in a very large ocean. It felt overwhelming.

Over the next few weeks, I worked hard to find the lay of the land – trying to fathom out where I fit in, in this big new world.

At some point, as I was working this all out something else occurred to me...

With the exception of Mr Morgan, the music teacher, *there were no other faces with brown skin like mine.*

## I'M DIFFERENT

My energy from that point on went into building a new persona. One where people didn't notice that I had different colour skin so that I didn't get singled out. I didn't want to be different, which I think is pretty normal at that age. I didn't want anyone to mention the fact that my colour was different to everyone else apart from Mr Morgan.

The new persona was very different from the young, innocent carefree girl who ran around the fields playing with her friends.

The 'new' me was way more interested in being the class clown. Not listening to the teacher in class, paying no attention to what I was being taught... more interested in getting the laughs and keeping everyone entertained. I created a tough exterior, one that said, "Don't mess with me..." which of course really translated to, "Don't mention the colour of my skin or that I'm different to you."

It was a full-time job for me, working on being one of the cool crowd. I was happy to compromise some of the values I had been raised with like respect, hard work and integrity, in order to fit in with my new cool friends. My entire friendship circle was renewed to fit into my too-cool-for-school new personality.

I would love to tell you at this point that it didn't affect my grades and that I turned myself around in school after a heart-warming and rallying speech from my parents and / or Hollywood movie style head teacher, telling me that I had so much potential that it would be a crying shame to waste.

But no.

The last bit is true – I was constantly told that I had a ton of potential and could be anything I wanted – but what I wanted was to remain cool, a bit scary and, ultimately, one of the in-crowd. Fitting in was supremely important and at that time, I couldn't see anything else that trumped it.

Some of these patterns followed me through my late teens, twenties and thirties – right up until I discovered NLP and learned how to accept myself exactly as I am.

Like many other people, I spent many years playing out the persona of the identity I actually believed myself to be, the person I had created so that nobody guessed I was different, or that if they did, they would be too scared to say so. This was all based on the story that I had told myself about what I perceived other people would be noticing and thinking. The fascinating thing to point out is that I had no evidence of anyone actually thinking this, or at the very least, of anyone indicating to me that I was different because of my skin.

It was my own new awareness of my skin colour and the meaning I put around it that created a fork in the road for me. I decided not to embrace who I was at the heart of me – happy-go-lucky, carefree and positive – instead choosing to be deceitful, not-giving-a-fuck, rebellious and focused only on what was important to me to stay cool.

> *"Wanting to be someone else is a waste of the person you are."*
>
> — MARILYN MONROE

We are always creating ourselves, whether we are doing that consciously or unconsciously. With each decision we make in our lives, each reaction, each conversation we have… we are always in the process of self-creation.

Now when you're creating yourself based on a false perception of yourself, from a place of not knowing your true values, your natural personality, the person you were before life gave you some of those battle scars... then you run the risk of creating yourself from a place of Fear. Back to the Ego or The False Self.

You're trying *not* to be something rather than being consciously aware of who you truly are and working towards being a better version of yourself.

---

"When you're working towards being a better version of yourself, first make sure that you know who 'yourself' actually is."

*Donna & Cheryl*

---

Wherever you're up to on your journey of knowing who your True Self is, you're exactly where you need to be. Right now, you're reading this book, doing this inner work because now is the right time for you. You don't have a DeLorean like Michael J Fox in the film Back To The Future to go back in time and redo your teenage years (and quite frankly, who the hell would want to go back to those years?) but from where you are now, you can work out who you are, what makes you happy and how you consciously want to *create yourself* from this second on.

## TIME TO KEEP IT REAL

Time to grab your journal. We want you to get close to your identity now.

When you ask yourself, 'Who Am I' – what comes up for you?

Who were you when you were a kid; what were you like?

What have you lost along the adulting journey?

## VALUES

This is the perfect time to talk to you about Values because we want you to challenge who you see yourself as and who you *believe* yourself to be. You've likely done values exercises before. We recommend you scrap what you think you know about you and go into this one with childlike curiosity of what your values are.

You may feel like you know them and you don't need to do this bit. This is where a bit of tough love comes in, Coach style.

It's our belief and experience that you have either:

1. Inherited your parents' values and so have been given your values without true exploration of whether they're actually yours.
2. Decided your values based on some of the crap you've experienced and what you *don't* want in your life.

So start from fresh. Once you have your values nailed, it makes so many of those day-to-day decisions, where you agonise over knowing the 'right' thing to do, so much easier. You have clarity on what's important to you. You have a set of guiding principles on which to base the framework of your relationships, parenting, work, priorities... and life! There is no part of your life that is not impacted by you not knowing your values or not living in alignment with them.

We are going to push you even further.

We don't want you to have a list of values as that can lead to more conflict and turmoil.

As they say in the movie *Highlander*, "There can be only one."

> *"Values are like fingerprints. Nobody's are the same, but you leave them all over everything you do."*
>
> — ELVIS PRESLEY

When you know your ONE overriding, overarching, ride or die value – the one that when the chips are down, *this one gets the final say* – then you have found your North Star. You can then always refer back to this one single value and use that as the bedrock of your decision making which is something our Soul Sisters in *The Real You* programme find makes that process so much easier.

## FREEDOM

One of our clients, Mel, experienced the power of this shift when she worked with us to get clarity on her life. She was feeling lost and pretty broken. She felt stuck in a job where her creative talents weren't recognised as she was 'getting through' life, most days having to coerce herself to get out of bed. From opening her eyes on a morning, she was filled with dread and overwhelmed with guilt that she was being a crappy parent because of it. She hated her job, hated her life and couldn't work out how she had got to this point.

She couldn't recall the last time she felt confident in herself or in her body – or in her life.

Her Imposter Syndrome was totally running the show, describing it as like a drill in her head from waking until she went to sleep, exhausted from the relentless inner turmoil. While she desired a life very different from the one she was living, she couldn't get herself out of the repeating pattern of self-sabotage fuelled by self-loathing. Her husband loved her to pieces, but from where she was at that time, she just couldn't accept that love because her own disgust towards herself overshadowed everything else.

In recent history she had had a successful business and her beautiful products had been in high end stores but due to some unforeseen circumstances, business had gone south and she was shouldering all of the blame. Mel saw this incredible venture and brand as her failure. She said she just hadn't been good enough.

In our first session we talked about her values, asking what she was committed to, and 'security' was way up there. Like many of us, her experience as a young woman hadn't always been plain sailing. There had been a few storms at sea. Her need for stability in her relationships had resulted in her belief that her core value was security. Her decisions reflected that. Keeping herself stuck in a job that, in her words, was suffocating her and feeling that she had no other option, was a strong piece of evidence.

For us it was clear that there was a disconnect between the value system she was operating her life under and her yet unknown truth.

## NORTH STAR

In that same session, we helped her identify what her true north star was. Her true core value was *freedom.*

Now I'm sure reading this, you can see that if you're operating from a place of having security as your driver compared to freedom, you're going to experience some significant discomfort, as they're pretty different.

Deep down, she wanted the ability to create, to travel, to maybe even have her own business again – although she was scared to admit that. Due to her being highly tuned in to her Inner Crazy Lady, she was utterly convinced that she would fail at any other business venture so there was no sense in leaving the job she had because she 'needed' the money and quite honestly... there was nothing more attractive to go to.

Her pain and discomfort in her life were from her operating outside of her core value. This internal struggle leads to us feel completely out of alignment and that manifests many problems. We can feel angry, frustrated, uncomfortable, unfulfilled, empty, lost, confused.

> *"Peace of mind comes when your life is in harmony with true principles and values and in no other way."*
>
> — STEPHEN COVEY

We asked her to put a pin in all of the stuff that she felt wasn't working out in her life just for five minutes and to step into what a life of 'freedom' meant for her. Where would she be? What would she be doing? What did she feel like in that life?

What we saw before us was the miracle of seeing someone start to listen to what their soul is whispering to them. Her whole body language changed as words of living abroad and being in the sunshine flowed from her tongue. Her eyes lit up as she described what it would be like to have her own business again where she could work from anywhere she chose, and she pictured herself sitting on a veranda in a beach house, sipping wine while the kids laughed and played on the beach.

Once she shifted her focus to basing her thoughts, decisions and actions around her core value, the game was changed.

- She quit her job because it wasn't bringing her joy and wouldn't help her towards her big goal of having her own business.
- She got a new business partner for her 'failed' business and breathed new life into it.
- She went on a TV programme looking for their dream house in the sun.
- She started up a new brand which she went into partnership with on some global deals.

She doesn't have a drill in her head any more. She's totally in flow with her zone of genius and she gets to create art, the thing she loves most, every single day.

This is the *power* of you knowing your North Star. It's not just something you whip out at corporate team events – it's a living and breathing part of you, whether you're aware of it or not.

## PUT A BIG FAT PIN IN IT

Just as dangerous as not knowing it, is what happens when you DO know it and decide to ignore it.

Think now about when you have had a boyfriend, job, friendship that went south. Cast your mind to what the breakdown was and we bet it will have a lot to do with very different value sets at play.

As women, we often put a pin in what's important to us in order to keep other people happy, so we can compromise our values to try to keep the peace or to try to 'save' a relationship. We have both worked for companies in the past where we didn't agree with the company values being played out and it doesn't feel good. Then you're effectively doing the job for money and having to leave your morals over to the side so that you don't rock the corporate boat. Once or twice you may get away with it but when you're doing this frequently, you lose respect for the company and you lose respect for yourself for staying there.

It's the same scenario in our close relationships. At times we have allowed lusty loins to override our inner inkling that maybe we aren't quite the best fit. Yes, we see you! We have all done it! Allowed our senses to completely block out the voice inside telling us that they're just not the right person for us. We prefer to live in denial and think that it's all going to be ok – or even worse, that we can fix the bits that aren't quite right – because when we are in love (or believe we are at the time) logic goes out the window.

Love, as they say, is a drug and it's a really potent one. There aren't many of us who haven't done some crazy shit at some point because of those feelings of infatuation.

---

"Know your worth and agree to never settle for anything less than you deserve again."
*Donna & Cheryl*

---

For some of us, we have compromised our values over a very long time, even years. So much so that you can't remember where it all started. You get lost in it and mostly then use it as another reason to beat up on yourself because none of us can be happy or like ourselves very much when we are not living in integrity with our values. It feels really shitty and is not a happy path.

## THE PAYOFF

So why do we do it? Well, at the beginning, when the love drug oxytocin is coursing mightily through your bloodstream and your hormones are on high alert, the void that you had of feeling not worthy or good enough is being filled to overflowing by the attention, words and actions of the other person.

We are allowing the other person to fill up our self-esteem cup and when we do that, the payoff for having that, of feeling loved, special, adored is greater than the need to stay within our values. Think of a time when you've compromised what you knew to be your values for this very reason. When you reflect back, you'll see that it wasn't because you forgot your values, you just at some level decided that putting a pin in them was worth it. We know that may feel tough to hear but like we said, we want to keep it real with you.

Eventually (when the drug wears off) we come to see that we *have* compromised our values, that we have nothing in common, that we disagree on some of the big issues.

You may be reading this and thinking, "Shit, that's me right now!" and if it is, that's ok. Awareness is a gift. You can choose whether to stay out of alignment with your values for the payoff or you can decide not to. Either way, it's about you doing it with a *conscious awareness* of the decisions you are making.

For you, it may actually be that you're compromising by putting a pin in your values at work. You may have a boss who has different ideas to you and doesn't run things how you would. The company values may be different to your core values. You may well feel like a square peg in a round hole. Your payoff of getting your pay cheque and having your perceived security is a higher value for you than working in true integrity with your core values.

Family is another minefield when it comes to your living in your truth whilst also trying to please others, keep the peace and prevent the ones we love feeling let down, stressed or seeing us as somehow different to how we were raised. We would rather sit in our own discomfort around some family conversations where views are being openly expressed by some and we hold back from speaking our truth. There are times when we keep ourselves small and compliant to what we believe our family expects from us or will tolerate, rather than rocking the good ship and having a man overboard situation, i.e. us!

In all of these situations, it is our need or want for external validation, for the approval, love and respect of others that trumps us standing up for our own values. And while we tell ourselves we are ok with it, as you will know from living through it... it just doesn't sit right. We ignore, bury, refuse to face the uncomfortable, icky feelings it gives us in the hope that the reasons we did it will make it all worthwhile.

It may in the short-term but it's highly unlikely to work as a long-term life strategy.

---

**TIME TO KEEP IT REAL**

What is your one core value, your personal North Star?

Where are you not living in your truth with this right now? Think of work, relationships, money and health as examples.

What inspired action do you want to take based on this new insight?

---

## BOUNDARIES

Boundaries are an actual thing… they are real, they're just not visible. They are the rules, limits or guidelines that we give to people around us to show them how to treat us, how to communicate and interact with us. Boundaries are invisible lines, just like a map that shows people where your borders are. If you don't tell people where the invisible lines are, then they're going to be drawing their own lines, based on their own maps.

Boundaries are everywhere, in all relationships and whether you created them or not, you're working with them all day long. Your job is to ensure that the lines you're operating in are the ones which make you feel safe, happy and in harmony with your life.

> *"It is necessary and even vital, to set standards for your life and the people you allow in it."*
>
> — MANDY HALE

Creating the Boundaries that make that happen for you is your responsibility. When you fail to do that and if you then don't make sure that those around you know where the lines are, what they are and how they work, then other people will create them for you. Much like belief systems, Boundaries are always in operation, whether you're consciously aware of them or not.

When you have a strong Belief System that you're worthy, good enough and know what you bring to any table, then your Boundaries are going to be strong, healthy and well communicated. They're doing the work for you! They will be making sure that your balance and inner peace are up front and centre and not being compromised because it's clear to all who know you what you stand for, what you don't stand for and how you operate. There's no confusion or grey areas.

And believe it or not, people do actually really like to know where they stand. Much like kids, having Boundaries helps us to feel safe.

## INTERNAL BOUNDARIES

Before you can even look at how you invite other people to engage with you, first comes the work on your Boundaries of how *you* treat you. Because that speaks louder than anything. It's super tough to ask someone to treat you with love, kindness and respect when you pay no regard to doing that for yourself.

Our clients in *The Real You* often realise when doing this work why creating Boundaries with others has been so challenging up until now - because their Internal Boundaries were lacking.

Your Internal Boundaries set the tone for the ones you'll echo in your relationships. The funny thing is that often we can lack these personal contracts with ourselves but actually get really uppity when other people simply reflect them back to us and deal with us in the same way! They're really only mirroring back what we are doing.

Here's a common example. You work bonkers hours, you answer emails within 0.01 nano-seconds of them coming in and then The Boss sends you a last minute email at 8pm about a big presentation that needs pulling together within 24 hours for The Head Honcho and you think, "How dare they, for God's sake? Do they not think I have a life? How's about a bit of notice? I'm not paid to work 24/7!"

Then you go do the presentation.

Guess who is going to get asked again in another two weeks when The Boss has another last minute life-or-death-ninety-nine-page-powerpoint-presentation-emergency? Yup. You're on speed dial, because you've already set the precedent and you know that you've done it more than once already.

Your lack of respect for your personal time and purposeful communication of your Boundaries creates mirror behaviour from the people around you. This is the rule, *not* the exception.

What you see around you in how you're being treated will likely be a reflection of how you're treating yourself based on those beliefs of *what you think you deserve and what you're worthy of.*

When it comes to your personal Boundaries there isn't a right or wrong way to do them. It's simply about designing those lines for yourself, wherever it is you want them to be. As the CEO of your life, you get to choose. You make the rules for you.

Here are some examples of Internal Boundaries:

- Speaking only kind words to yourself
- Eating food that nourishes your body daily
- Getting enough sleep
- Deciding you stop work at 6pm
- Choosing to take a lunch break
- Abstaining from social media an hour before bed
- Putting your phone away when you're having quality family time
- Taking a holiday and spending time doing what you want to
- Looking after your body
- Setting up and sticking to agreed family budgets
- Using social media only to feel good
- Turning off the news

- Scheduling You time in your diary regularly
- Daily routines that give you a ton of energy
- Saying no to things you don't really want to do
- Being *The Real You* in every life situation
- Demonstrating your core values to yourself first
- Filling your day and life with work, activities and people that bring you joy

Each area of your life requires you to have an unwritten contract about how you choose to show up for yourself in that area. We encourage you now to get really clear on what those non-negotiable Boundaries are for you, because when you have that clarity it makes daily life a much smoother ride as your decisions have been made up front. That means less energy wasted on questioning yourself, trying to work out the best thing to do, feeling guilty or beating yourself up. More energy to be focused, fun and playing full out in your life. Doesn't that sound like a better way to live?

## EXTERNAL BOUNDARIES

Just as with your Internal Boundaries, your External ones are for you to decide. Nobody can do this for you. And look, we aren't here to turn you into a sociopathic cold-hearted bitch who doesn't give two toots about other people, nope. The principles are to support you to have healthier, happier, more open relationships in all aspects of your life. You being you is the best gift you can give yourself and the people who love you.

> *"It's important to understand that setting boundaries isn't a way to get rid of people, but a way to keep them in your life without destroying your inner peace."*
>
> — VEX KING

Here are some examples of External Boundaries:

- Telling your team you're taking a lunch break
- Taking your parents shopping when it works for you and them, not just them
- Saying 'No' when you don't really want to go to the party
- Letting your family know you're having a no phone day
- Taking a weekly break from social media
- Setting expectations with your Boss on timescales for project delivery
- Choosing which friendship circles you spend your time with
- Limiting time to people who you find are mood-hoovers
- Telling someone you're not ok with how they're behaving towards you
- Informing your friends you're not drinking on the night out
- Saying 'No' to your Mam's death-by-chocolate cake when you're going sugar free
- Discussing with The Boss your travel and work priorities to find your balance
- Telling your hubby that you're going to go and read rather than watch more Netflix
- Taking an hour away from the kids to do your yoga or read House Beautiful
- Negotiating the salary which reflects what you bring to the table

## TIME TO KEEP IT REAL

Time to go back to your Book Resources at www.therealyoumethod.com/book-resources now and do the exercise on your Internal and External Boundaries.

When you have done both, look at both sets of results – what are the patterns and parallels?

What is the biggest insight you're taking away from the exercise? Note that here…

## BOUNDARY BLOCKERS

So if Boundaries are so amazing then why the hell *don't* we have them? Whenever we coach on this topic to our clients in *The Real You*, invariably the answer is, "Oh my God! I have NO Boundaries!" And that's not true, of course. There will always be some

Boundaries in place but they're usually not consciously created or they've been implemented after you've blown up at someone for taking advantage of you one too many times.

We have a saying in the UK, "Do I have 'MUG' written on my forehead?" which translated means, "Is there an invitation for you to ask me anything and expect me to happily crack on and do that thing for you?"

In short, the answer to that is often, "Yes!" because we haven't communicated with those around us what we expect and how we expect to be treated. Yet we get so pissed off when we think people are abusing our good nature.

If we ask you why you don't have Boundaries, the answer is often, "I don't like conflict!" which of course is going to be a big blocker if you correlate communicating how you want to be treated with a fight. We see ourselves as People Pleasers and instinctively then we recoil from the thought of being open and transparent with our needs. That's way too uncomfortable for us.

> *"I must undertake to love myself and to respect myself as though my very life depends upon self-love and self-respect."*
>
> — MAYA ANGELOU

Avoiding conflict is one of the most common reasons we fail to have Boundaries. Here are some other common ones:

- We don't know it's a thing to have Boundaries in the first place
- We are scared of what would happen if we had them – we may lose friends, people might not like us or they might ask us who the hell we think we are

- It's the path of least resistance; it's just easier to keep other people happy
- We don't want to rock the boat
- Change is uncomfortable and we avoid it like the plague
- The unknown is scary; we have never done it so how will it work out?
- We have never had them, so is it worth all of the hassle in the first place?
- The payoff for not having them is greater – people like me the way I am so why bother?
- Not having them makes it easier for things to be someone else's fault
- It can be easier to stay in victim mode and have less responsibility for our relationships
- We don't have them because then we would have to be consistent, and that takes work
- Sitting and hoping it gets better, taking the path of least resistance just feels safer

When we first met Nina, who headed up a successful record label, she was a poster child for burnout. She was exhausted, emotional, drained and completely spent after working flat out for years in a high-pressure, stress fuelled, competitive global role at exec level. She had hit the wall. She was what we would describe in technical coaching terms as, 'Fucked'. It is always painful to see a client at this level of utter physical, emotional and spiritual depletion. They have literally got nothing left in the tank and yet they are somehow managing to show up and keep going, but the toll it is taking on their health and wellbeing is scary.

She was trying to do it all. Work across countries with her team in a different country to her base, be a Mam to two growing children, support her Hubby in his new business venture, settle into a new home after moving country, find a new permanent home, sell their existing home, launch her new product, grow her 'baby' (her company)... and then somewhere at the bottom of the list, was her. Her self-care didn't even factor with so much other stuff going on in life.

She wasn't getting enough rest; she wasn't doing yoga any more; she wasn't eating well and was just grabbing whatever sugar based snacks she could get; she felt totally disconnected from her feminine power; she was travelling so much that she felt she was being a bad parent, but when she wasn't with her team she felt she was neglecting them – and the cycle of constant guilt had her feeling highly anxious every day.

For Nina, she couldn't see a way out other than just to walk out on the job that she loved so much – or had loved but was rapidly falling out of love with. She was burned.

Our priority was to get to work with Nina on her Internal Boundaries, starting with small acts of self-love each day to create more harmony and peace *inside*, before we could focus on the outside stuff.

She created a new morning routine with just a basic five minute meditation and then some journaling – no phone, email or work permitted for at least two hours upon waking.

Immediately, she felt the benefits of this. This created a different energy for her to take into her day. Feeling this success, it propelled her to introduce more changes. She committed to eating well in the day to fuel her energy more, and to going to bed earlier to get better sleep when she was travelling.

Soon she started on the External Boundaries. Starting small, it was shortening some meetings in the day so that she had ten or fifteen minutes in between to take a breather and regroup before her next session. Then she started saying, "No, thank you," to some of the post-work socialising, feeling less obliged and less guilty doing so. Then she started to reduce her travel, trusting she could manage her team wherever she was based. She gave herself permission to then take an hour at the start of her day to do yoga or go for a run, knowing she would be so much more productive during the day for doing so.

All of these small incremental changes added up to a huge, compound effect. Huge. Within months she was in love with her job again. She felt like a better parent as she was more present. Her relationship with her Hubby felt better than it had in years. She loved her body and had started embracing her feminine energy again. She was totally killing it at the record label and the usual politics that you get in any company just didn't impact her any more – and she had started to focus on some long term big life goals and had a clear vision of where her life was taking her.

> *"Nothing has changed but everything has changed."*
>
> — SOUL SISTER - NINA

She told us that she felt happier than she had in as long as she could remember and she recalled how she wasn't sure how she had been able to carry on 'as broken', in her words, as she had for so long. She hadn't had to do anything drastic to make huge improvements in her life. Her experience ultimately was the same but *how* she now chose to live that experience was completely different.

Many small, incremental changes and micro decisions every day lead to gigantic, seismic shifts in happiness, balance and wellbeing.

Nina went on to sell her old home, buy her dream home, get a huge raise and go on the holiday of a lifetime with her family where she was able to relax, be present and pinch herself at how joy-filled her life truly is.

*This* is the power of Boundaries.

## CHAPTER SUMMARY

- Reconnect to your younger self and remember that sense of fun and belief that anything is possible.
- You are always creating yourself and you are a powerful, limitless being with the whole Universe on your side.
- Work out your one core value, your North Star, then make your decisions and live your life with it at the epicentre.
- The payoff for compromising on your value is rarely worth it.
- Empower yourself with strong Internal and External Boundaries to enable fulfilling relationships and demonstrate self-love.
- Small decisions and actions will have a huge compound effect on your results.

**My aha moment from this chapter is:**

# 8

# YOU ALREADY HAVE EVERYTHING YOU NEED

> *"You are very powerful, provided you know how powerful you are."*
>
> — YOGI BHAJAN

## Cheryl

I was sitting with a gynaecological consultant after several years of being prodded, poked and injected with hormones in an effort to get my lady problems in check. It had been the most prolonged and challenging health experience in my life to date and it had been far from fun. I had a giant fibroid the size of a five-month pregnancy and it was uncomfortable to say the least. I was constantly bloated, swollen and actually looked pregnant, which made me feel self-conscious and particularly unattractive, wearing baggy clothes to try to disguise it. But here we were, having a conversation in which the consultant informed me it was the 'end of the line'.

Years earlier they had casually floated past me the idea that it would just be easier to have a hysterectomy but as I was only in my early forties, that felt a tad drastic to me. So I allowed them to try out other things in order to avoid surgery which included forcing my body into early menopause. Side effects of my treatments included anaemia, fatigue, nausea, hot sweats, disrupted sleep, skin problems, stomach upsets... the list goes on! All of this was in an effort to avoid going under the knife.

*Yet here we were again.*

Here's a summary of how the conversation went.

Consultant: How old are you?

Me: 44.

Consultant: Are you planning on having any more children?

Me: No.

Consultant: Well then, just have the hysterectomy.

Me: Why don't you get your cock chopped off?

Ok, so the last bit was only in my head.

But I'm fairly certain that my face conveyed what I was thinking. To him, having surgery to remove the offending anatomy seemed to be the most logical course of action. He's a surgeon. Their instinct is to cut. I'm not. My instinct is to stay in one piece and heal. Again, I just couldn't accept what he was saying and I couldn't help but think that if we were offering to chop off his manhood to resolve the issue, he would be keen to explore alternatives too.

I decided to pay for a private consultation with yet another consultant. I would love to say that because I was parting with more money that people sat up and paid attention that I was serious about finding a non-surgical alternative but no. Same answer from that guy too – have your insides removed. Well, that's how I heard it anyway.

> *"You must train your intuition – you must trust the small voice inside you which tells you exactly what to say, what to decide."*
>
> — INGRID BERGMAN

## INTUITION

I felt frustrated, angry and at a loss. I didn't know what to do next and the 'experts' were giving me advice that I just couldn't accept. My family and friends were all just echoing the doctors and saying, "Just whip it out!" and I knew they were worried and after years of seeing me in pain and struggling, they wanted me to feel back to normal again. But I couldn't explain it. I knew for me, that it just was not the right course of action. It felt totally extreme to me to take out a whole part of my anatomy, just because there was something wrong with it. I knew that doing that wasn't going to fix the root cause of what was going on internally.

I knew I had to take matters into my own hands so I decided to learn all I could about my condition. I started to read all I could about natural healing and made it a priority find a way of feeling better and helping my body with what was going on that didn't involve having a part of it removed.

Soon after I started working with a naturopath who I felt a great connection with and after running more detailed tests on my hormones, I started a specialised plan to change my lifestyle and heal my body from the inside out. My goal was to get my condition under control but along the way over the years, I have learned and gained so much more than I could ever have predicted about myself, my body, my energy and the mind, body and soul connection. I now know how to nourish my body, how to listen to my body and how to give it what it needs.

Now look – I'm not saying here that you should go and tell your doctor to go screw themselves. Not at all. What I'm saying is that *you have a say*. You know your body better than any doctor ever could. When you have a niggle, a small quiet voice giving you some inside info, then don't ignore it just because some guy in a white coat with a fancy qualification walks in a room. In this case we are talking about doctors but I know that you get what I'm saying here: the doctor could be an estate agent, a financial advisor, a solicitor, a police officer... whatever the scenario, if you have something chirping away at you giving you opposing counsel, hear it out and ask the questions you need to until you're satisfied.

---

"Your intuition is priceless so ffs listen to what it has to say."
*Donna & Cheryl*

---

My intuition guided me on a journey which has radically changed my life and that intuition made it pretty easy to get *radically committed* to whatever action I had to take in order to create the shift I wanted – which was to feel good in my body again and to avoid surgery. I am happy to report that my health over the last three years feels as good as it ever did and now I have a new appreciation for the body I inhabit and how miraculous it is. It also led me on the path to becoming a Pranic Healer. So listen to your intuition: it has so much to offer and insight that you would happily pay someone else bloody good money for!

## INNER GPS

We all have Intuition, an Inner GPS that is always working to guide you to whatever it knows is the best path for you to take. Most of us, however, tend to ignore it and go with the flow based on things like what we think other people will think, what other people advise us to do or what seems like the right thing to do based on what we can see in that moment. That little feeling that is niggling away at us, trying to get us to go in another direction, is ignored because it doesn't have facts to back it up. It doesn't make sense so we find it hard to give it credibility because it doesn't have a logical argument or clear reasoning to it.

> *"The more you trust your intuition, the more empowered you become. The stronger you become. And the happier you become."*
>
> — GISELE BÜNDCHEN

From when we are kids, we are told to rely more on what our five senses of touch, sight, taste, smell and hearing are telling us, rather than what our woo-woo sixth sense is leaning us toward. We are taught to not have faith in something that can't really be seen or explained and to stick with what can't be argued with right in front of our eyes.

Seeing is believing, right?

Well, it's dangerous territory to get into because your sixth sense is there for a reason. In our experience, when you turn down the volume or ignore it completely, there's often a price to pay.

Let us bring this to life for you with some personal examples from us. See which ones you can relate to:

1. You're interviewing someone for a role in your team. The CV is great; they have all of the experience you have asked for and then some. They are answering all of the questions with an A+ response and every word is like a phrase from the company handbook. BUT something just isn't clicking. You have the niggle. But you can't not hire them based on your niggle so you go ahead, offer them the job, and within a month you're regretting that decision because the thing you couldn't put your finger on is playing out in them not performing as they ought to based on their CV. There are issues that you need to deal with and you know this person isn't the right person for your team.
2. You meet THE guy. He's gorgeous, got a great job, treats you like a queen, your friends love him. BUT you have that niggle. Despite them saying all of the right things, your spidey senses are telling you that something is off. You then find out that whilst on the surface everything was like a romantic Sunday afternoon movie, he's actually already married. Yup. There's the niggle now biting you on the ass.
3. You have a big project kick off at work. All of the data is pointing you to a certain course of action which seems the most sensible with the biggest return and has the greatest impact. BUT something keeps niggling at you that maybe this isn't the best course of action. You

> plough ahead with the plan because all of the numbers stack up that this is the right thing to do. Before you can say 'low-hanging fruit', you're knee deep in project problems, delays and a very frustrated stakeholder group... and you can now see what your niggle was all about.

We bet you can sit for ten minutes and easily rattle off twenty occasions when you've ignored the niggle and quickly lived to regret it! We simply aren't brought up to tune in to, amplify, trust that gut instinct of ours. We aren't trained on what a beautiful gift it is or informed that this higher faculty we are all bestowed with is always working towards your highest good. Your Intuition has become an additional piece of info that is easily cast aside.

## YOUR HIGHEST GOOD

It takes real courage to act on your gut. To fly in the face of facts, figures and people's opinions to stand for something that evidentially doesn't stack up. In Cheryl's story, it wasn't always easy to be confronted with friends and family who wanted her to follow the doctor's recommendations and to feel judged for not going with the expert opinions. It's not a popular path to follow, going it alone. It can feel lonely and isolating to not be understood. Trusting that your Inner GPS is working in your best interests, always with the goal of your highest good and knowing the whole picture, takes practice and faith.

As we write our book it's three years since we set up our business, Now Is Your Time. When we announced that we were leaving our corporate careers to set up our online coaching business as women in our forties with zero digital or entrepreneurial experience between us, we don't mind telling you there were more worried frowns than there were gung-ho cheerleaders.

"How is that going to pay the bills?"

"Do people even hire Coaches?"

"Don't you have to have a special qualification?"

"Surely you won't make the same money as you did in corporate?"

"Is that even a thing? Who wants to be coached online?"

"Isn't that only an American thing? Life Coaching?"

"How long will you give it before you go back to your normal job?"

"Aren't you terrified of failing?"

"Isn't coaching a totally saturated market? Everyone is a Coach now, right?"

"Seriously, who would pay for that?"

"Wouldn't you be better just sticking to what you know?"

Don't get us wrong, all of these people had good intentions. They didn't want us to be bankrupt, homeless or worse still – failures. We are from a particularly risk averse, working class background and we tend to follow in the footsteps of the generations before us. There weren't people in our lineage that were doing what we said we wanted to do.

> *"Have the courage to follow your heart and intuition. They somehow know what you truly want to become."*
>
> — STEVE JOBS

But our Intuition on this was so strong, so sure, so loud that we simply were not able to ignore it. In the face of all that worry, concern, advice to stick with what we knew, our Inner GPS told us that we had to forge ahead. Our third year of business was in the global pandemic of COVID - yet we still trebled our business, expanded our team and generated over $500,000 revenue in that year alone.

Not too bad for two middle aged women without a clue how to set up a business.

That's why we say, *believing is seeing.*

Learn how to tap into this Inner GPS, develop your faith in it and create a relationship with it that isn't disdain or ignorance but is instead collaborative and harmonised. When you have a two-way relationship with your Intuition, life feels so much more in flow because you're not fighting against yourself. You're not trying to suppress the nagging feeling that something isn't in alignment for you. You can embrace the guidance, get to where you want to go faster because your Intuition is downloading all the info from The Universe so it knows more than your five senses alone can grasp.

## TUNING IN TO YOUR INNER GPS

Ok great, we have you on board but now you're desperate to know how the hell to tune in to your magical inner Goddess that has all of this great advice, aren't you? And why wouldn't you be? Learning how to tune in is one of the greatest gifts you can give yourself so we are going to share our favourite ways with you right now so that you can get in on the action.

### 1. Go In

When you have a problem or a question that needs answering, you've learned over the years to ask for advice, to canvass opinion about the 'right' thing for you to do next. We like to have the consensus from our friends on what they think about the thing at hand and what we really, really, really want is their seal of approval on what is usually our proposal (rather than our decision) about what we plan to do. You don't trust yourself to make that decision without lots of input. Work on asking yourself what *you* feel (not just think) is the right next action in an area of your life that you want some upward movement in. And go with that.

### 2. Develop Faith

Even when you have a knowing of what is right for you, there are times when you've gone with the general opinion instead, haven't you? To develop a relationship of trust with your Intuition, you have got to give it a chance to show you how unbelievably talented it is! Give it a chance to show you what it's made of, let it show off a little, give it room to take centre stage; and trust us, you'll want front row tickets every time. Listen to it, act upon it and allow it room to grow. Like any relationship, it's a two-way street. Open up the lines of communication and get committed to this being one of the most fundamental relationships in your life.

### 3. Journaling

You'll love this one because you get an excuse to go treat yourself to more new stationery. Now, we don't want you to get too hung up on how to journal 'properly'. There are no laws about the right and wrong way to do this; it's about what feels good to you and remember that this is about you tuning in and developing your relationship with your Inner GPS. Grab yourself fifteen minutes and a quiet place to sit (or if you have a family, whack your headphones in and blank them out for a bit) then with your posh new pad, choose an area of your life that you want to work on and ask yourself what your Intuition knows. See what comes up. Ask yourself some questions like:

- How do I feel about this area of my life?
- What improvements would I love to see?
- Where would I love to be twelve months from now?
- What would my Intuition have me do next?
- What does my Intuition want me to do more of?

If those questions don't feel aligned, ignore them! Sit and just let the pen flow. You may sit and nothing flows and all you can think about is the laundry, the fact that you're out of dog biscuits or how you forgot to book the plumber for the dripping tap... that's all just your busy-mind responses to being still. Trust the process and believe that you have something that you really want to hear and ignore your inbuilt resistance to tuning in.

> *"When you don't know what to do, do nothing. Get quiet so you can hear the still, small voice - your inner GPS guiding you to true North."*
>
> — OPRAH

### 4. Meditation

Much like journaling, there isn't a right or wrong way to meditate. And it's not about stopping your thoughts, which is pretty much impossible unless you're at Deepak Chopra level of meditation. For most of us, this is simply about learning to calm the mind, and to create space for some inner focus and a channel for allowing The Universe to drop in some golden nuggets of wisdom for us to respond to.

When you're always on the go, getting shit done and hustling yourself into a frenzy, it can be pretty hard to hear any of the whispers or see any of the flashing neon signs our Intuition is trying to show us. When you're meditating, it takes down the volume on life so that you have a far better chance at hearing something other than the Crazy Lady between your ears. You get to turn up the volume on the whisper.

Whether you listen to a guided meditation on YouTube or you invest in Headspace (which we love) or you just find a quiet spot in your day and sit for five minutes, we highly recommend that you build in the practice of meditation into your day. If you would like our help then we have created a super simple guided five minute meditation for you in your Book Resources which you can use to help you get started.

Go to www.therealyoumethod.com/book-resources and give it a go!

If even that feels like too much hard work, then try this.

Sit somewhere comfortable where you won't be disturbed.

Close your eyes and take a few deep breaths.

On the in-breath count one.

On the out-breath count two.

Breath in, three.

Out, four.

Keep going until you get to ten, then start again.

Repeat a few times, then take another few deep breaths.

If any thoughts pop in your head just go back to your count.

If you lose track, start again at one.

There you go; you just meditated!

However you choose to do it, this is all about just getting into the moment and out of stressing about yesterday's presentation to The Boss that didn't go to plan and out of future-tripping about tomorrow's meetings that you don't feel prepared enough for. Get into this beautiful, perfect, present moment and know it's all going to be fabulous.

**5. Create Space**

What the hell does creating space mean? Well, just giving yourself some room away from your normal daily stuff that needs doing in order to have a bit of room to gather your thoughts. Giving yourself a change of environment works wonders as it immediately shifts your energy. Our favourite thing to do is to take a walk on the beach as it always helps us to think more clearly and it's frequently where we have our more inspired ideas.

Going into your garden, taking a walk, going for a run, stroking the dog, cooking, having a bath or shower, drawing, driving... anything where your busy mind goes a little quiet and allows for your Intuition to get a word in – to be able to *hear*.

As you're in the activity, be relaxed, be in that moment and if you have a particular question you would like the answer to, then ask it and let it go into the ether, trusting that your answer is going to make an appearance at the perfect time. No need to force it or try to work it out, but go back to your activity and believe that your answer is on its way. Then listen for clues or signs because things will start popping up!

---

## TIME TO KEEP IT REAL

What steps are you now radically committing to taking in order to build your relationship with your Inner GPS?

Note them here...

---

## SUPERPOWERS

We grow up watching our Superheroes flex their superhuman super-strengths in order to save the planet. They are an elite species of half human, half genetically modified beings who can do things that are impossible for the normal human. They're untouchable, usually gorgeous looking and often have a tendency to wear their underwear as outerwear.

So when we ask our clients, "What's your Superpower?" we never get a straight answer. We get blushes, hair twiddling, awkward shuffling in chairs, blank faces and sometimes, tears.

Nobody just owns their shit and says, "I am brilliant at helping people see their potential," on the first pass.

And why would you? You're not sitting there with your underwear on over your jeans. But it's our belief that each and every single one of us has at least one Superpower.

Yes, that means you too.

We know that you're probably super squirmy right now and potentially thinking that we believe that because we don't know you and you're the exception. But honestly, we won't be budged, and we can't wait to get your email one day telling us that we were right! For now, we want you just to suspend your disbelief and go with us on this one. We promise it will all be worth it soon.

> *"We can change the world if we change ourselves. We just need to get hold of the old patterns of thinking and dealing with things and start listening to our inner voices and trusting our own superpowers."*
>
> — NINA HAGEN

You see, a Superpower doesn't mean that you can fly, be invisible, climb vertical buildings with your bare hands, stretch to two hundred times your normal size, see through stone, make fire turn to ice or any of that stuff. What Superpowers really are, are those qualities that you have that you naturally do that you haven't had to work hard on, you didn't need a certificate for or didn't have to go to Uni to learn. It's your gift. It's the thing that you do which comes easily to you and other people probably compliment you on and it's unique because quite frankly – there's only one you. So how you do it is there for a one off. There has never been and will never be another you and your gift.

Just let that sink in for a moment.

There has never been another you with your gift and there never will be. Not ever.

---

"The Universe created you in absolute perfection so stop worrying about the size of your ass."

*Donna & Cheryl*

---

**YOU'RE A ONE OFF**

Your Superpower is an instinctive ability you have and right now you may or may not be using it. Our desire for you is that you don't only identify this Superpower but that you *use* it regularly in your daily life. The crazy thing is that in many cases, because we don't recognise or appreciate our Superpower and we spend an exorbitant amount of time working on the stuff that we think we *aren't* good at, we have often created a whole career to the exclusion of this amazing ability.

Our energy gets channelled into getting stuff we aren't naturally brilliant at up to par and when people ask what we are working on, the answer is usually the stuff we are trying to fix! Imagine just for a second a world where everyone was working in their Superpower area and only ever focusing on enhancing that skill. How bloody brilliant would that be?

Everybody using their natural gifts and bringing those to the planet every day – you wouldn't need to create Superheroes! The energy on the planet would be off the scale! Holy shitballs.

Here are some Superpowers that our clients have remembered they had when working with us:

- Gift of the gab (gab = mouth and this phrase means you can chat to anyone)
- Making people feel safe
- Seeing opportunities
- Picking up on people's energy and what they need
- Making people smile
- Speaking up for those with no voice
- Creating change in society
- Writing captivating stories
- Painting beautiful pictures
- Designing brands
- Being strong leaders
- Helping people get healthy
- Being kind and compassionate
- Loving unconditionally
- Making people laugh
- Showing people how to accept and love themselves
- Building teams where people flourish
- Listening
- Guiding people to find their purpose
- Playing music
- Entertaining
- Reading a room and creating connections
- Empowering women to know their finances
- Taking photographs

- Designing clothes
- Showing children how to understand their emotions
- Developing new drugs
- Teaching spirituality

## TIME TO KEEP IT REAL

Now it's your turn.

You're going to claim your Superpower and start tapping into it to make your life more fun, more fulfilling and a whole lot easier by using your unique gift.

My Superpower is...

**Donna**

When we are stressed, we tend not to tune in to our Inner GPS and Superpowers can fly out of the window. Like in this personal example...

One sunny Saturday afternoon, I was in the park with Kaleb who was around three at the time. He was screaming at me, "Higher,

higher Mammy!" as all kids do at that age. He loved those swings and the butterflies feeling you get when you swoosh down. Having that time with him was so precious. I think as an older Mam I appreciated these moments so much as having a baby had been a real miracle for us after four years of trying to conceive. A simple trip to the park on a Saturday morning for me was (and still is) a joyous thing and particularly at that time because I worked away from home through the week so I felt like I missed out on so much of normal life with him.

Then my phone started ringing. I looked down and my heart sank. Fuck, it was The Boss.

I stepped away from the swing because I didn't want him to hear the squeals of delight coming from Kaleb and the other kids because I felt guilty that I was in the park. Yes, it was a Saturday and I felt guilty for being in the park with my son and I was worried that he would be irritated by the kids screaming. WTF.

## BALANCE

I took the call hoping it would be something quick and easy that I could hand to the team. As the call started to go on, I could hear Kaleb demanding louder and louder that I push him and he started to squirm and wriggle in the swing chair. I was torn between continuing to listen to my irate boss and going back to make sure Kaleb didn't split his head open trying to get out of the swing.

Finally, the call with The Boss was over and I was left with a shit-stinking-hum-dinger-urgent issue that had to be fixed pronto. Against his will, I forced Kaleb to get back into his pushchair because I now had no time to dawdle back home looking at flowers and clouds in the sky. I had to hit the phone on my stomp back home, apologising for the sound of my screaming child who was frustrated at being whipped away from the park before he had even had his ice cream.

I spent the rest of that Saturday on the phone, resolving the issue with my team and feeling overwhelmed with Mam-guilt that yet again I had ruined our time together. I felt angry, resentful and frustrated, knowing that tomorrow night I would be packing my bags again ready to leave home before he was up on Monday morning.

I would love to say this was an exception but it was not. And what I would tell myself was that this was the price I paid for the great salary I received and the life I had created for my family.

This was the sacrifice.

I know this story will resonate with a lot of working Mams who are trying to prove that they can be it all and do it all. Looking back now, I see how badly I was burning my energy reserves out, experiencing a total lack of balance – but if you had asked me, I would have said that I took great care of myself, that I ate well, trained, meditated and I would have also said that I loved my job.

## POWERING THROUGH

For years I had been running at this speed. Working twelve-hour days away from home, getting home and trying to cram a whole week into a weekend. When I did have a week on holiday I would literally not want to speak to a single person if I could help it. My phone was always welded to my hand (and my phone was a

Blackberry for many years, which I still miss!). I ran 24/7 operational centres so being on call at crazy hours came with the job.

The thing is, we aren't built to work at the pace many of us work in the sustained way we do for as long as we now do. Work has become a relentless energy sucker – in my mind I think of it as a bit like the Dementors in Harry Potter – where our actual life force feels like it's being drained from us for double the number of hours a week that we are actually contracted to work.

I had been *powering through* for years, doing just enough to keep myself from crashing. I actually remember being excited to go in for a major operation because I knew it meant I would get a break – how fucked up is that? I never admitted at that time that I was burnt out, but I was. My life was played out and timed in seconds and every single second had to have a diary slot and a purpose.

There was no time to just be. And as human 'be-ings' that is something we all crave, but I would feel tremendous guilt if I didn't spend any free time I had with Kaleb or The Hubby or with my family because I 'should' spend more time with them to make up for the fact I worked away all week.

This epidemic of guilt, of feeling like we should constantly be 'on', is a stress-packed, testosterone-fuelled happiness thief which devours more and more of us and is never satiated.

Until we stop, make different choices and live our life with the reverence it deserves as the miracle that it is, we won't get off the hamster wheel. Every day we are making life choices and decisions that ultimately will culminate in our day of reckoning. At that point will we ask for another few days with our loved ones? Will we wish we had taken better care of ourselves? Or will we be there wishing we had worked harder and earned more money? Not likely.

Whatever it is that you want to do with your life experience, it will be more fun and fulfilling when you decide to power up rather than power through.

## SELF-CARE ISN'T SELFISH

You are in charge of your energy and of creating the energy that is required for you to have the life that you desire. It is NOT selfish to take care of yourself. It is sensible. You want to be there for your family, your friends, your team? Then you have got to start taking care of yourself like you would a top performing athlete. Because that's exactly what you are. Your life is a marathon and a series of sprints. You're in this for the long haul so if you get burned out in the phase you're at now, then worst case scenario, you won't actually be around to help any of the people you feel depend on you right now.

---

"You have to be your own knight...
you have to rescue your fucking self."
*Donna & Cheryl*

---

Bottom line – stress is a killer and the creator of dis-ease within your body. Your goal has to be not just to avoid it but to actively help your body to heal and the best way it knows to do that is when it's in a state of happiness. We could blind you with all of the stats on this but the proof is out there for you to read –

happiness isn't just a nice to have, it's essential for a healthy body!

You're using energy all day long. And much like your mobile phone, your battery needs to be topped up throughout the day. Energy is created by you and if you want to be at the top of your game of life, you'd best make sure that creating energy is top of your list of things to do each day.

Here are some ways to create energy daily:

- Eat well
- Rest plenty
- Get seven to eight hours' sleep
- Drink a couple of litres of water
- Take regular breaks
- Meditate
- Listen to music
- Have a two-minute dance
- Stand in fresh air
- Read something that inspires you
- Listen to a podcast
- Journal your thoughts
- Exercise
- Stroke your pet
- Call a friend
- Laugh
- Go for a walk
- Take a shower
- Watch something funny
- Put your phone away
- Look at some old photos
- Connect to your vision

- Write down your Gratitudes
- Do a random act of kindness
- Lie and watch the clouds float by

## POWERING UP

There are a million ways you can recharge your battery throughout the day; the trick is making sure that you are consciously aware of this and remembering to do it in the day. Have a daily intention to make creating your energy a daily priority and put reminders in your calendar or phone for every hour to prompt you into action. Don't leave this one to chance because you will get sucked into your day and before you know it your battery will be bleeping at you at bedtime! Then you will fall into an exhausted sleep, promising to do better the next day. Until you create a new habit with this, make it easy with plenty of reminders.

---

"Self-care isn't just spa days and meditation.
It's saying no, having boundaries and watching
Netflix in your pjs in the middle of the day."
*Donna & Cheryl*

---

Creating energy has to be a priority for you to make some changes and start taking premium care of yourself. Your desire to look after yourself has to be greater than your excuses around not having enough time, not having the money, not having the energy or the discipline in the first place. We hear you; we have used all of those excuses too. But because we love you and we want the very best for you, we are happy to call you out on your bullshit and tell you that's exactly what those things are. Excuses. You've decided that you're not a priority enough to make yourself the priority.

If you stick with the excuses, you're going to get more of what you currently have. If you switch, then you have the opportunity to have so much more to give of yourself to those people you love so much – and more importantly, you get to enjoy this one and only experience in this body.

---

## TIME TO KEEP IT REAL

My self-care commitment to me is....

---

## CHAPTER SUMMARY

- Your Intuition is priceless and is always available to you.
- Invest in this relationship with your Inner GPS as it is always guiding you to your highest good.
- Embrace your unique Superpower and make the world a better place by using it daily.
- You are responsible for generating your energy and it's your most valuable asset.

- Stress is toxic to your body so feeling good isn't a nice to have, it's essential.
- Self-care isn't selfish, it's sensible.
- Get radically committed to powering up instead of powering through.

**My aha moment from this chapter is:**

9

# YOU ARE THE CEO OF YOUR LIFE

> *"I do not fix problems, I fix my thinking. Then the problems take care of themselves."*
>
> — LOUISE HAY

**Donna**

The first 'proper job' I had was straight after university when I started working in a contact centre for a telecoms company. I got the job within days of leaving, so sadly didn't get to party hard for the summer after finishing my exams, but my working class roots had me feeling driven to get a job immediately as I couldn't possibly sit around doing nothing! I started as agency staff and I was made permanent soon after and honestly, I felt like I had won the Lotto. Going from counting the pennies (actually literally counting pennies for bus fare at points) to suddenly receiving a really great salary felt *amazing*!

Soon there was an opportunity to go for a leadership role within my team. I had worked so hard, learned a ton and I felt like I had a really strong chance of getting the role because of the feedback I had got from my manager at that time. I prepped hard for the interview, thought of examples for every possible scenario, learned the company mission by heart, had mock interviews, prepared a portfolio of successes – I left no stone unturned. I was going for it, all in. I was also absolutely shitting myself and felt totally exposed but it felt like fate. *The role had my name all over it.*

I went out shopping, got myself a new suit and I was ready. There were even shoulder pads. Bring. It. On.

My interviewers were two senior women in the company and I admired both of them massively. They were both role models of the kind of leader I aspired to be. I wanted to do a great job to show them how much of an impact their mentoring had had on me since joining their organisation. It was my chance to shine! During the interview I answered all of the questions they threw at me in textbook style. I felt like this was *my* moment. It was all falling into place. I may well have been bordering on smug as I relayed to my friends that night how well the interview had gone – I had even managed to keep my cool and not lose my thread when one of them had a rather unexpected and messy nose bleed in the middle of it. I was on fire!

The next week I was invited to a meeting for the interview results. I was so excited! I was wondering which team I would be given, what shift pattern I would be on and of course... what salary uplift I would be rewarded with! I had my acceptance speech all planned and I couldn't wait to thank them both for all of their help in making me one of the youngest and fastest internal promotions ever in the history of the company. *I was ready.*

In I went, all smiles and blushes and giddy. After they asked me how I felt the interview had gone, they dropped the bombshell that I *wasn't* the successful applicant.

The 'No' isn't 'never' they told me, I just needed more time to get some more experience and stronger examples.

Fuck. Me. Hard.

I was completely and utterly gobsmacked.

More experience? Stronger examples? I had thrown everything I had at them and I still wasn't enough.

Ouch.

> *"Reject rejection! If someone says no, just say NEXT."*
>
> — JACK CANFIELD

**MESSY MELTDOWN**

I can't really remember much else of what was said. I had this awful, swirling, swooshing thing going on in my ears and I was battling the urge not to throw up all over their fancy shoes.

I felt like a complete idiot, a fool and like I had been hung out to dry. Everyone was going to be laughing at me.

I would have to leave and look for another job. I was washed up at twenty-three with no hope of ever being a leader like they were.

It would be a fair appraisal to say that I didn't take it well. The 'No' felt personal. I wasn't worthy enough for this role, for this company.

*I wasn't good enough.*

As I sat home that night, all washed up with my bottle of wine and box of Maltesers, I thought of my bleak future and felt overwhelmed that all these dreams I had of leading people and teams were all flushed down the loo. My world felt sad and I didn't know what I would do next. All my hard work had been for nothing. If I wasn't good enough now then I wouldn't be good enough in six months' or six years' time.

All of that, from the word, '*No*'.

I put all of this meaning on it, I vetoed all of their feedback about my potential, my growth, my future with the company because all I could hear in my head was the word, 'No'.

## THE BIG LITTLE WORD... NO

Now, we know as you're reading this you will have your own examples flying around your head of when you have heard the same teeny tiny word and have spiralled into a Bridget Jones style night in with wine and chocolate, singing Celine Dion at the top of your lungs. Maybe for you it was a No from a lover. Maybe it was a No from your parents for something. Perhaps a friend said No to a night out. Was it a client you made a proposal to and they said, "No"? Maybe you asked your two-year-old son if he loves you and he said, "No" (yes, that happened too!) or it could have been a job scenario for you too.

Bottom line: we hear that word and what is really going on is... REJECTION.

There. We said it!

We are all scared of being rejected. Of not belonging, of not feeling *good enough*.

The word 'No' has become a word of such gargantuan importance and fear to us; we react so strongly to hearing it because of the meaning we pour into it from the store house of limiting beliefs, trauma, negative experiences and life events that we have stockpiled so far. Now it's time to break that down – to remove the heat, the fear, the horror of the word.

What does this miniscule word *actually* mean?

It means:

*Not from that person*
*Not for that thing*
*Not at that time*

When you affirm this formula to yourself the next time you hear the word No, it will stop you from going down the rabbit hole of creating a whole fairy tale about what it means about you, to you or for you. It puts a circuit break in between the response you just got and the negative momentum you would usually start creating.

Put it in your phone, save it somewhere and commit it to memory so that the next time you're on the end of a 'No', you don't waste hours or even days locked away, licking your wounds and gaining 10lbs from eating Ben and Jerry's. It just means *not from that person, not for that thing, not at that time.*

For most of us, No is a double-edged sword.

## TAKING BACK YOUR NO

We don't only not like hearing it… we aren't too fond of *saying* it either. We are as crap at saying it as we are at being on the receiving end. That's because the same rules apply. We inject it with collagen! We plump it up to bursting point with the filler of what we think the other person will hear when we say the word, 'No'.

Our perception of what us saying 'No' means to the world:

- I don't like you
- I'm a mean bitch
- I don't care
- I'm a heartless cow
- I'm more important than you
- I don't know how to do something
- I'm better than you
- I'm scared to do it
- I'm high maintenance
- I'm arrogant
- I don't want this opportunity
- I want confrontation
- It's all about me
- I'm selfish

This is People Pleaser *hell*! Which one on this list is the one that jumps out at you? Which one does your Crazy Lady scream at you when you're brazen enough to consider saying, 'No' to a request? We would rather walk around feeling done-to, victimised, like the whole world is on our shoulders, rather than womaning-up and saying 'No'.

Write this down...

"No is always a complete sentence."
*Donna & Cheryl*

## WHO'S A SELFISH BITCH?

The mere thought of saying, 'No' to The Boss, our mother, our friends, can bring us out in sweaty palms, palpitations and sleepless nights. The conclusion is drawn quickly that there is going to be a confrontation of sorts where we are called out and shamed for being awful, selfish bitches. This confrontation is to be avoided at all costs, so it's best just to suck it up, buttercup and keep saying, 'Yes' to all of the shit that you don't have any real desire to do.

*Newsflash* – living that way totally sucks so get skilled, confident and happy at exercising your right to say, 'No' when that's what you as a grownup wants to do. It's time to put those big girl pants on (and you have our permission to do that under your clothes instead of Linda Carter style) and say what it is you actually mean.

No.

If you want to go wild and add something to it, you can consider adding a, 'Thank you' at the end. Anything other than that isn't required. There is no reason for you to *justify* to anyone your reasons. There is no requirement for a sales pitch to ensure the other person is bought into your No. And get this.

The other person doesn't have to agree with you.

*Mic drop.*

We get that it's super uncomfortable to imagine not having people on board with your decisions but the truth is that you don't *need* permission or approval from anyone other than yourself.

---

"To become the CEO of your life you have got to get comfortable with hearing NO, saying NO and not needing everyone to agree with you."
*Donna & Cheryl*

---

Say your, 'No', own it, stand in it and be completely at peace with it. All you need to do is practise using it to get to that stage. The next time you're invited somewhere you really don't want to go and you have your usual urge to say, "Yes sure, I would love that!" and what you're saying on the inside is, "Jesus H Fucking Christ! I wanted to have a hot bath, wear no makeup and veg out in my pjs with no bra.." - Stop, take a deep breath, smile and simply say, "No."

> *"The difference between successful people and really successful people is that the really successful people say no to almost everything."*
>
> — WARREN BUFFETT

Nobody is going to come along and do this one for you. But we know that you can totally do this. Start small. Think of somewhere in your life you know you say, 'Yes' when what you want to say is, 'No' and mentally rehearse it going the way you want it to next time. We promise you it is THE most liberating feeling and if you're really set on creating those Boundaries we talked about, sooner or later, you're going to need to put this card into play.

You will find that people still love you and while occasionally people may choose to question your No, you decide whether or not you want to elaborate. The more you do it, the more confident you will become and it gets easier and easier. You've got this!

---

### TIME TO KEEP IT REAL

Where are you making a story out of hearing No?

Where are you saying Yes when you really want to say No in life?

Journal on these questions and decide what inspired action you're ready to take and note that here:

---

## THE EXPECTATIONS GAP

Life would be so much simpler if everyone did what they were supposed to do. If the Hubby would only clear up the empty toilet roll holders from the bathroom. If he knew that there is a right way to clean the house and that isn't to hoover before you dust. If that driver this morning had not cut you up. If The Boss was more proactive and organised about what he needs from you. If your clients didn't change their mind about what they wanted. If the government didn't keep making ridiculous decisions. If the kids would just behave the way you wanted them to...

---

> "Your life is what your thoughts make of it."
> *Donna & Cheryl*

---

We can drive ourselves out of our minds with anger, frustration and confusion wanting people, events and life to be something other than they are. We can have relationships with people for decades and still be frustrated that they do something a certain way, which pisses us off *every single time* they do it. We chat to our friends, sharing our utter disbelief at something The Other Half did at the weekend, completely flabbergasted at their actions... when actually it's the same thing they've been doing for at least the last two decades of knowing them. But still, we expect different behaviour.

And of course, we are in the right and they're wrong. Goes without saying.

We like to be right and to hear our friend tell us that she would feel exactly the same and would 100% be equally frustrated by a man who doesn't understand the concept of a recycling bin for used toilet roll holders. What a joke! Definitely grounds for a divorce.

> *"Most people want to get what they want, whereas the secret is to want what you get at this moment."*
>
> — ECKHART TOLLE

Every day of our lives, we are losing our shit over stuff that we think should be one way – *our way* – when it is the way it is. Our thinking is usually around what we would do if we were them, if we were in that situation, and we judge them accordingly. We are driving ourselves absolutely bonkers, complaining about the outturn of life and wanting it to be something other than it is. The desire for people, situations and life to be a certain way gets in the way of our happiness and ability to go with the flow.

## SEEKING VALIDATION

This kind of thinking rarely brings out the best in us. Our judgement that something or someone isn't what it's *supposed* to be, usually creates the need in us to share this less than happy experience and what we usually want from sharing it, is to be agreed with. We for sure aren't usually telling our friend the tale of woe of the husband who doesn't clear up empty toilet roll holders, for her to tell you that he's a really great guy and maybe you're being a little dramatic about the whole thing.

No! You want her to *agree* with you so that you can feel righteous and share that 'everybody' thinks the same as you when you confront him about his out of control toilet roll behaviour whilst having dinner tonight. You want confirmation of your position. You want to hear that *you are right*.

Which effectively, makes them wrong.

The danger with thinking this way in terms or right and wrong, is that it makes it highly unlikely that you're going to happily come down from your tower in order to hear what the other party has to say. You're only listening – if you're willing to listen at all – from the perspective of believing that there is a right and wrong and that you've already snapped up the right one, so from that point forward, all conversations come fully loaded.

## PERSPECTIVE IS EVERYTHING

When we want something or someone to be the way that we desire, our field of vision narrows, our perspective goes AWOL and our Ego takes control. And by Ego we mean that shadow part of you, the False Self, the one that is always hungry and in need of feeding. It is fed by resentment, fear and all the other low vibe energy that doesn't make you feel good. It's totally insatiable and when it is in control, it's a great red flag to know that a different course of action is required because the Ego isn't coming from the place of your Higher Self.

> *"That which offends you only weakens you. Being offended creates the same destructive energy that offended you in the first place so transcend your ego and stay in peace."*
>
> — DR WAYNE DYER

In life, when you feel that you're wanting something to be different from how it is, then it's a great universal nudge to check in with yourself on what's really going on for you. Because under all of the noise of anger, frustration, indignation, upset, toys-out-of-pram-throwing... there is a Belief System being triggered that is creating the thoughts that something should be different to how it is, which is creating the feelings you're experiencing.

---

**TIME TO KEEP IT REAL**

Where in your life are you doing this right now?

Where do you want your relationships to be something they're not?

How do you want your job or business to be different than it is?
When it comes to your finances, how is this showing up?

And what about your health?

Grab a cuppa, journal on these questions and make your list before you move on.

---

It's important for your sanity that you work out a way to get ok with things being as they are. Not in a way that you just throw your cards in the air with a, "Fuck it!" mentality. That's not ever going to work out well for you in terms of getting you closer to the happy, fulfilled, expansive life you want. It doesn't mean that you don't set Boundaries and have conversations that need to be had.

Look at that list of yours and work out for each of the items on it, what it's going to take for you to not be at war with that part of your life.

What's the conversation you need to have?

What Boundaries do you need to set?

What expectation do you just need to let go of?

## LET THAT SHIT GO

To be the CEO of your life, it takes awareness and commitment to creating seismic shifts from being a person who is always allowing their happiness to take a kick to the crotch because of how things around them are panning out, to being someone who doesn't give their power away and knows how to be in the moment but not necessarily *in the emotion.* You have got to get 100% committed to being in charge and responsible for your own emotions, which come from your thoughts and your Belief System. Nobody, repeat nobody can 'make' you feel a certain way. As tempting as it may be to apportion that kind of blame, sadly, it just doesn't stick. That buck stops with you.

> *"Expectation is the root of all heartache."*
>
> — WILLIAM SHAKESPEARE

Take that knowledge and power that comes with it and use it to fuel a calmer approach to your life where you are truly in control through regulating your expectations. Whether it's your Mother-

In-Law always ringing when your fave programme comes on or a global pandemic – how you *expect* it to be is in your control and whatever happens outside of your control, isn't going to be persuaded to behave differently and time won't be turned back just because *you're* not happy about the way shit went down.

We promise you that when you let go of expecting life to go as you would wish for it to, whether that's the small or the big stuff, and you get into the flow of acceptance of it just exactly as it is in this moment, you will feel so much freer, lighter and more also more supported by The Universe herself. *Let that shit go,* know that it's all happening exactly as it's supposed to and get into identifying what your next right move is from a space of good vibes only.

---

"Everything is happening exactly as it's supposed to, so stop wishing for things to be different than they are."
*Donna & Cheryl*

---

## BOUNCEBACKABILITY

### Cheryl

I love a get together with the girls – they're the best form of therapy I know. We go on breaks together every year to get our 'fix' of girl time. But on one particular day in August 2019, I was getting an extra slice of them in a pub, in a way I could never have anticipated. Just over a year after my Dad passed and we set up Now Is Your Time, my brother Christopher died suddenly and unexpectedly. It was a shock to us as you can imagine, especially to my Mam – we couldn't begin to get our heads around how this felt for her.

Here we were again, the girls there for support at another wake for a close family member.

"Is this how we catch up these days?" I said to the girls. Even in the darkest of times, there was something to be grateful for and it felt good to lighten the mood just a little.

They all laughed. "We just said exactly the same thing!"

Losing both my Dad and brother in consecutive years was challenging to say the least. Just because I have a ton of mindset strategies up my sleeve, doesn't mean I find the process any easier. It still was loss, tragedy and pain both to experience and to witness. Putting a positivity plaster on pain – pretending everything is ok, looking on the bright side, brushing it under the carpet because of how uncomfortable it feels – isn't the goal.

> *"Even though all these obstacles keep coming at you, you just have to keep going through them."*
>
> — DIANE KEATON

That's not how we create mental resilience, or as we love to call it, Bouncebackability.

Bouncebackability isn't about avoiding your feelings. We know from working with our clients all over the world in *The Real You*, that this is a common misconception.

It's the opposite – it's about feeling ALL of the feels because *that's* how you create mental resilience. There's a perception that mental resilience is about getting over stuff really quickly and escaping from it unscathed and untouched. Like it had never happened.

Hollie had even bought me a mug years ago saying, 'Shut up and deal with it.' I was well known for my no-nonsense approach to life. I didn't believe in wallowing, just keep moving forward and don't stop to look back. I thought I was doing great...

Actually, what was happening was that I wasn't really dealing with *anything.*

I was emotionally lugging around the baggage of all the stuff I'd swept under the carpet over the years. And it was heavy.

It wasn't until my mid-thirties when the epiphany hit me that I wasn't 'dealing' with anything. I was moving around it, side-stepping it. Suppressing it so that I *didn't have to feel* it. Years of dusting myself down and powering through took their toll on me.

## EMOTIONAL BYPASS

When I became consciously aware of the fact that I hadn't been *allowing* myself to feel the feelings for all of those years, I was gobsmacked. That's about the best word to describe it. Gobsmacked. I had formed the belief that I just didn't feel stuff. I was a bit like 'The Terminator'. I just kept on going. I got the job done! Then... boom. I had ALL of the feelings and I realised how my identity of being someone who just builds a bridge and gets over it, had become so much my reality for so long that I didn't question it any more. I had become that person so that I could deal with life and I had stopped learning how to *emotionally process* life.

Swallowing down my feelings had been my way of processing them the best I knew how. What I now understand is that I was actually bypassing my feelings for fear of what they might do to me.

The fear of our feelings – especially those big emotions like grief, rejection, upset, sadness – has us running scared from them. We don't like to sit in them. They don't feel good! We are scared that they'll overwhelm us and we won't come up for air again from them... so we do our best to avoid them. This won't be a conscious decision because our subconscious mind is always working to keep us safe, so if it senses something scary, it's going to have us running in the other direction.

> *"People who wade into discomfort and tell the truth about their stories are the real badasses."*
>
> — BRENÉ BROWN

**LEARNING TO FEEL**

This leads to us not knowing how to deal with them when they come along. I didn't express my feelings and I realised that I hadn't taught my daughter, Hollie, how to express her feelings either. When she would experience her big emotions, I would do my best to put the positivity plaster on to move her past it quickly! I hated seeing her upset so thought I was doing the right thing.

I had no idea that I was teaching her how to *avoid* her emotions. But as I didn't know how to deal with my own, I sure as hell had no idea how to explain to her how to deal with hers either.

As I learned that my emotions were trying to teach me things and were there for a reason, I had to learn how to allow them space and honour their purpose. I had to be brave and start to let them bubble up. Even my language had to change. If someone would ask me what I felt about something by way of an opinion, I would respond with what I thought about it. I had to get conscious and start asking myself what I felt, really felt about things in day-to-day life. I had to *learn* how to tune in to how I felt; it wasn't something that came naturally to me because I had untrained myself completely from this way of being.

By the time it came to dealing with the grief of losing my Dad and brother, I knew it was important for me to feel all of the emotions that come hand in hand with grief. All of those big, dark, scary and deeply uncomfortable emotions that take you on a feeling roller coaster when someone you love dies.

Sometimes, you've just got to *sit in the shit.*

Those big emotions hit their peak, they reach their musical crescendo where it feels like they're going to drown you and then they start to ebb. They loosen their grip, they start to calm and you can start to breathe again.

In all of life's masterclasses, you have a choice not about the external events which go on, but you get to choose how you *experience* your experience.

> *"In any situation, you have the right, power and ability to choose your experience."*
>
> — IYANLA VANZANT

This is life. *Shit gets messy.* But you always have a choice of how you decide to experience it and that comes down to your *perception* of what's going on. I was undeniably sad to have these two people I loved not be in my life any more but the reality was that no amount of my sadness would bring them back into our lives in the same human form. For me, staying in that amount of sadness wasn't an option. It didn't feel good to me to only think about the shocking and traumatic moments of those events. I chose to focus on the lifetime of other memories I had to fall back on. That's not always easy but it is a choice.

When a wave of emotion would hit me from a song or a smell, I would allow it, give it permission to have its moment and then as soon as I felt it subside, I would reach for a memory of something that made me smile and I would give my focus to that. My goal would be not to ignore my emotions but not to be a victim to them because ultimately, we are the ones who are creating them from our beliefs and thoughts. So if I had sat around at home all day thinking of how awful and tragic, hideous, unfair and heart-breaking it all was, I may still be in the house to this day in my pjs, watching Game of Thrones, drinking tea and eating biscuits.

But I get to choose my experience.

I choose each day even now to focus on the good memories and if the wave comes because of a memory, a date, a place or I hear bagpipes (Dad's favourites) I still choose to allow the emotion room to process and then choose again a thought that brings me back to my usual, happy, peaceful state.

> *"Pain is not tragic. Pain is magic. Suffering is tragic. Suffering is what happens when we avoid pain and consequently miss our own becoming. That is what I can and must avoid: missing my own evolution because I am too afraid to surrender to the process."*
>
> — GLENNON DOYLE

## CHOOSE AGAIN

Choosing again is one of the greatest tools you have in your mindset toolkit and as a CEO, you can always rely on this one when you need it. It doesn't matter what scenario crops up in your daily life that you need to practise your Bouncebackability from – an unexpected letter from the taxman, a parking ticket, a health issue, a disagreement with your partner, a house move falling through, the kids driving you nuts by leaving dishes everywhere, the dog throwing up on the new carpet – whatever it is, you have the power in your mind to choose a different thought, a different perspective in order to come back to feeling happy and good on the inside.

---

"Life will keep Life-ing but you get to choose how you experience it. That's all you."
*Donna & Cheryl*

---

Your goal is to feel good as often as you can, for as long as you can. When your other feelings pop up, check in on what thoughts are going through your head because that's where they are originating from. Then you can decide what you want to choose in that moment. You can be in control of what experience you are going to experience at that point in time. This is how we grow, develop and get confident in our own unique Bounceback-ability.

## TIME TO KEEP IT REAL

Over to you now.

Knowing how to create some Bouncebackability in your life is essential for you to be happy and healthy.

Head over now to your Book Resources at www.therealyoumethod.com/book-resources where we have a great exercise to help you get clarity on where this is holding you back and steps on how to start nailing it.

## CHAPTER SUMMARY

- No is just a word; it's the meaning you're putting around it that is making it bigger than it is.
- No just means not from that person, not for that thing, not at that time.
- You saying no to other people doesn't make you a bitch, it makes you honest.
- Letting go of needing people, situations and life to be the way you want them to be, rather than just what they are, will allow you more happiness and peace.
- Judging people makes you feel low vibe and is handing your power away.
- Bouncebackability comes from processing our emotions and feeling all the feels.
- Life is messy and shit happens but you always get to decide how you experience it.

**My aha moment from this chapter is:**

# 10

# LIVING AS YOUR HIGHEST SELF

> *"True power comes from standing in your truth and walking your own path."*
>
> — ELIZABETH GILBERT

## Cheryl

I was sitting in the kitchen at HQ early December 2018, six months into our business, with my head in my hands crying. I had just received a text message from my Hubby, Graham, to say the tenant was moving out of the flat they rented from us. Now ordinarily, I would say, "Okay, that's a shame, we'll find a new one and everything will turn out as it's meant to. We may have to tighten our belts a bit in the meantime..." but not today.

The money I had borrowed from my Mam to cover our bills for the last three months had run out, I didn't know how we were going to pay the bills the following month and it was my daughter, Hollie's 21st birthday the week after! And Christmas was looming over me which I hadn't saved for like I normally would have. Now we had to pay two mortgages until we found another tenant.

This text message tipped me over the fucking edge.

## WHY IS IT NOT WORKING?

My mouth immediately went dry, I started having palpitations, feeling sweaty... to say I went into a state of high alert anxiety is an understatement!

Yes, I may have slipped into victim mode for a moment, thinking, "WTF; anything else?"

Donna was looking at me surprised by the emotion as I normally put my positivity pants on and see the silver lining in any situation and respond in a much calmer way. She was trying to talk me down but I wouldn't let her get a word in edgeways.

I mean, every day I was saying my daily affirmations, focusing on gratitude; I was meditating consistently, reading self-development books every day – God damn it! I was being of service to women around the world so why the fuck was this happening to me?

I thought to myself, "Clearly all of the work I'm doing isn't working. I must be doing something wrong for this to happen. I'm obviously getting in my own way and stopping the business from growing as I'm trying to manifest money and instead I'm creating more money issues. I've been doing all of this daily mindset work consistently since we set up the business so why isn't it working?"

I was ready to throw in the towel. Going back to corporate and getting a real job, the security of a monthly salary never seemed more attractive. If I just got a new job in January then I would be able to pay the bills and this would solve all of our problems.

Basically, I was acting like the sky was falling down and then I had a word with myself... and Donna stepped in to stop me spiralling.

And remember we told you...The Thing Is Never The Thing.

This had nothing to do with the tenant moving out. It may have been the catalyst but it was not The Thing.

The Thing really was The Guilt.

The Guilt of knowing that it was the decision Donna and I had made whilst sitting around the same table six months earlier to set up our own business that had led us to this point where for the first time in a very long time I was worried about money and the pressure that was putting on my Hubby too. I was stressing about how my putting my desire of having a business ahead of how the hell I would pay for lovely gifts for my one and only daughter's 21st birthday. I felt guilty that at my age, I had borrowed money from my Mam. Surely by now it should have been the other way around and I should be treating her!

The Guilt that I had been doing a dance with since we had jumped into this adventure felt like it was going to swallow me whole. Donna and I didn't really discuss setting up Now Is Your Time with our other halves. We were so all in from the first conversation we had about it, we bulldozed rather than discussing. We told, rather than asking for any kind of agreement and we expected them to go wholeheartedly along with our plan. Which wasn't particularly well formed, we grant you that!

So when this teeny tiny setback of running out of money and the tenant moving out appeared, then The Guilt just couldn't be sidestepped any more. I felt like I had put my happiness ahead of our security and all of a sudden, I felt vulnerable, exposed and something I wasn't used to feeling. Doubt.

## THE GRIP

It didn't feel good. It's not a familiar feeling for me. I'm blindingly optimistic as a default. My faith and knowing is solid. This unsettling emotion in my body felt completely out of my natural alignment. In that moment I felt completely rocked.

I was completely in The Grip.

> *"Nothing ever goes away until it teaches us what we need to know."*
>
> — PEMA CHODRON

These moments will come up for you just as they did for me and just as they did for Donna as we have talked about in previous chapters. Once you set universal wheels in motion and get busy creating your dream life, you don't get a free pass from having some bumps in the road. These things are your tests. They are universal assignments from The Universe, sent to check out how committed you really are to this new path of yours. You'll often find they pop up just as you're embarking on a new venture or project. You've said you're all in, so how all in are you when the shit hits the fan?

When your head is all over the place and you've started to spiral, you can't just switch it off. It's started to gather some emotional momentum because of where your thoughts are heading so you've got to do what we call... 'get the bad out'.

Have you seen the TV programme, This Is Us? If you haven't, you're missing out and if you have, you'll know this trick.

In that show, there is a husband and wife team called Randall and Beth. When something happens in their lives that freaks them out, they take turns voicing all the things they think are going to happen because of it. They get it all out. For example, they have a foster daughter at one point and they realise they don't know what they have got themselves into. Randall does his run down ending in the fact that she may kill them all in their sleep that night. And Beth doesn't judge. She just gives him her run down too.

It's a great way of just getting all that bad crap in your head out, hearing how out there it sounds and you then don't even have to do anything with it! But by not keeping it in your body, by giving it permission to air and just be what it is, it can actually stop the momentum in its tracks. This means that you can get back into neutral quickly. You see, you can't go from being up a height, white-knuckling the situation to being totally zen and ok with it. Once you've gone, or started to go up, you have got to give it some space and honour it enough to exit your body.

Pretending you're ok is not a strategy, like we said in the last chapter.

## WHAT'S THE STORY

Donna asked me what the story was I was telling myself. She got me to list out all of the crazy that was going on in my head, all the way through to Graham leaving me for being so selfish because we had lost our home due to my midlife-crisis-business failing and we were living in a tent on the local beach.

It shifted my energy. As I was saying it, I realised how crazy it sounded. I also realised I was saying things like, "We have NO money, there's NOTHING I can do, we're doing all this work and we've made NO progress... it's all a WASTE of time!"

When we say these words, we can hear back how powerless we are sounding and how we are standing in that victim energy. We can also hear and identify that it's just not true!

The evidence to back up those statements was missing.

---

"Your words create your world."
*Donna & Cheryl*

---

I did have money and had ways to access money. Things were tight and it wasn't going to be our most lavish Christmas but we were by no means on the breadline.

There was a lot I could do, including looking for a new tenant.

The only real waste of time was spending any longer in this energy which was not moving me closer to my goals. Coming back into alignment was THE biggest thing I could do at that moment. Energising the emotions that I didn't want to feel would only create more of the same. What I wanted to feel was happy, trusting it was all working out – which is my normal aligned state.

> *"You can change your world by changing your words... Remember, death and life are in the power of the tongue."*
>
> — JOEL OSTEEN

## HANDING IT OVER

Now that I had loosened the grip emotionally, it was time to reconnect to the knowing and faith that we had always relied on through the journey so far:

That we were here for a reason.

That our calling to do this was so strong that I would be taken care of.

That if my energy went into how I could serve the world with my gifts and talents, by the Law of the Universe I would be financially compensated.

That I'm always being guided.

That even when I can't see it, there's a plan bigger and greater than the one I have which is always working out for my highest good.

The Universe has got me covered.

We call this spiritual surrender. Being in the faith of knowing it's all in hand and forgetting about any kind of control that we think we have and going back into that place of just trusting and knowing.

I'm not saying it's always easy! I was a control freak for a long time and I was exceptional at it. But truth be told, it's bloody hard work and even with the best of intentions, there are other universal factors at play. My journey to understanding this has not been smooth sailing but it has been the most awakening and enlightening of my life.

It has been a key factor in recent years of getting me through times just like these and when I've felt I had to grab hold of the reins and start driving hard then actually the thing I really need to do is step away. I hand over whatever happens next to that universal power far greater than I can comprehend and have total faith that it's going to get sorted out exactly as it should in divine timing.

Life lessons like your tenant moving out just before Christmas with your daughter's 21st pending are great opportunities to build trust and faith in that knowing!

> *"Live life as if everything is rigged in your favour."*
>
> — RUMI

**COMING BACK HOME**

Reminding myself of our big vision made me start to feel good again and then doing a run down of all of the things right there in that moment that I had to be grateful for, brought me back home. And by that I mean into my inner space of joy and peace.

I headed to my actual physical home after doing this work and as I walked through the door I collected the mail. When I got to the kitchen I had the urge to open it which I wouldn't normally do straight away.

There in a nondescript white envelope was an unexpected cheque from my bank for £2000.

Yep. Crazy right? All my bills were taken care of for another month.

The Universe really does work in mysterious ways and they're far more advanced than my teeny human brain can ever fathom so I don't worry myself with working these things out. I just trust and know that it always does.

Here are your Five Steps to Come Back Home – to recover your inner peace and alignment.

1. What's the story you're telling yourself?
2. Get the bad out – download all the inner crazy talk.
3. Do a reality check – what's the fact versus the fiction?
4. Remind yourself of your BIG goal and your Why.
5. Get your vibe back up with your Gratitude Overload.

## TIME TO KEEP IT REAL

Where in your life right now are you feeling out of control?

Pick one area you feel you are you white-knuckling it.

Take ten minutes and complete the five step process to coming back home.

Journal what comes up for you.

## RAISE YOUR VIBE

It may be that your goal in buying this book was to find the silver bullet of eternal inner peace and self-confidence that is totally unbreakable, unshakeable and endures all.

If that's so, you may want to ask for your money back.

There isn't a book in the world that can give you that. Sure, we can give you the tools, tell you the techniques and strategies but, keeping it real (as by now you're pretty clear that we do), it always boils down to you implementing those things consistently. That's because we are all human and you forget about how utterly brilliant, beautiful and powerful you are.

It's easy to get swept away in the daily stresses and strains of life, allowing the problems you're faced with to become bigger than The Real You, the Goddess, the divine shining light that you are.

Your job every single day of your life is to come back to that truth, to remind yourself of your limitless, unstoppable power and potential.

The tendency to only do the things that make you feel good when you already feel great, is real. Our clients in The Real You have shared this with us so many times. They feel amazing when they're taking great care of themselves – working out, eating well, journaling, meditating, having fun – then the proverbial shit hits the fan in terms of a project blowing up or someone getting ill in the family... and all those good habits go to the wall.

They start eating crap, having a few glasses of wine to relax, don't have time to work out because they have to power through, they can't make time for fun because they feel guilty, they stay up late, drinking the wine and eating the chocolate in order to have a bit of 'me' time... you recognise the pattern, right?

> *"Knowing others is intelligence; knowing yourself is true wisdom. Mastering others is strength; mastering yourself is true power."*
>
> — LAOZI

Does doing any of that stuff make you feel better? Maybe it does in the moment. We are generally wired for immediate gratification so don't be too hard on yourself if you nodded along to the whole list. We know because we used to do the same on a weekly basis!

Here's the big fat BUT: it does not serve you.

Then on top of the existing problem, you feel tired, sluggish, annoyed that you did it in the first place, blah blah. We know you get it and honestly, we aren't asking you to become a sugar free teetotaller who goes to bed at 8pm. (But all power to you if you do, we haven't managed that yet!)

What we are inviting you to do right now is to build some daily spiritual habits which help you raise your vibe, connect you to your goals and have you feeling happy each day. It may not be all day every day, but when you apply your daily practices with consistency, you'll be shocked at how good and energised you can feel despite whatever problems you see going on.

"It's impossible to pour from an empty wine bottle."
*Donna & Cheryl*

These problems will always seem bigger when you're tired, frazzled and depleted. That's when the fear has an open door to walk through. It's easier for the anxiety to turn into overwhelm and for the Inner Crazy Lady to start really going to town and telling you how useless you are. When you haven't been taking care of yourself, you haven't got the manpower to have the guards ready to deal with her and before you know it, the only voice you can hear is hers.

The Real You struggles to take back control when it's gone this far and your defences are already in the dust.

AND... the good stuff was showing up more often when you felt great because that's what you were attracting into your life with your high vibe state. It wasn't a coincidence!

## GET RADICALLY COMMITTED TO YOU

The bottom line is for you to be the best version of you, to be able to live life as the highest expression of yourself, you have to prioritise your daily spiritual practice. Build these habits into your daily routine so it just becomes something you do every day like brushing your teeth.

If becoming the best version of you is something that you're committed to being, then just reading about it in this book or the next isn't enough. You have got to get radically committed.

All through this journey with us, we have encouraged you to take action. We have told you how important energy is, so we would love you to build into your day the things that are going to help you raise your vibration. There are a ton of books on morning routines and you're welcome to go read them, but our guidance for what it's worth is to keep it simple and fun. It should be something you look forward to daily, not another thing on the list of 'How To Be Perfect' to check off.

---

"When you know who you really are and what you really want, you become unfuckwithable."
*Donna & Cheryl*

---

Creating not only a morning but also an evening practice that bookends your day beautifully so that you are consciously generating the emotional state you want to be in, gives you a massive leg up on the daily spiritual practice ladder. Your mind is most open to suggestion first and last thing as your brainwaves are in a more relaxed state, so they're more open to suggestion.

It's a great mindset hack. You can imprint on your subconscious mind much more easily at those times of day. This makes it easier for you to impress the commands, thoughts and beliefs that you want so that you're writing, producing and directing the movie of your life that you get to star in.

In the old days, we would jump out of bed, eat, get ready and jump in the car to get to work. After working a long day, an evening would consist of shopping, cooking, TV and falling into bed exhausted – ready to rinse and repeat the next day. Over the years as we learned from our spiritual mentors and our coaches the importance of having a daily spiritual practice, it has become one of the most valuable, loved and treasured parts of our day, as it does for our Soul Sisters in The Real You.

When we first were invited to implement a morning practice, our response was: a) I'm not getting up at 5am and b) Are you freaking kidding?! We barely have time to eat on a morning never mind do all of this!"

Change curve, you could call it.

We remember our Coach, Niyc Pidgeon, smiling and saying to us, "Trust me, this is the one thing that when you feel the power of it, you won't ever want to give up."

Girl was right.

## FIND YOUR OWN GROOVE

Whilst we had both tried different things over the years as more of a fad, neither of us had consistently had a routine that was all about energy. The daily practice we were now being taught was all about getting your whole self, mind, body and spirit into alignment with who you are, your purpose and power every single day. You go about the business of consciously creating the energy that you want to embody for the day ahead.

It doesn't have to take hours. You can create something that fits you and your lifestyle and your family. But you have to want to do it and at first you may be doing it because we've suggested it but soon you too will get it and will be a convert.

As one of our clients in The Real You Online said, "Yesterday I woke up feeling tired, fed up and snappy... didn't do my morning affirmations or gratitudes... had a shit day. Business was slow and 'Felicia' was running wild and free in my head. Today I woke feeling tired, said my affirmations and gratitudes out loud, gave myself and Felicia a talking to and I've had a busy day at work, chatted with colleagues and came home feeling strong... starting to see a connection!"

> *"There is a great substance within each present moment, just waiting to explode with goodness, magic and blessings."*
>
> — PAM GROUT

We are sure you've worked it out, but 'Felicia' is this client's Inner Crazy Lady. This is the power of having a morning practice because you get to decide how your day is going to be. Then you can inform The Universe and remember, she only ever wants to say, "Yes!" to you!

Here are some of our favourite things to incorporate into your daily practice – try them, see what feels good for you, have fun with them. Experiment. There's no right or wrong, only what makes you feel good and raises your vibration.

### Morning Practice Ideas

- Smile when you wake, before you even open your eyes.
- Gratitudes – list anything you feel glad for in that moment.
- Affirmations – state them as if you're already there in the "I am".
- Meditation – even a few minutes will be great and 15-20 even better.

- Breathwork – counting or even just being aware of your breath.
- Intention Setting – decide how your day is going to be and declare it.
- Visualisation – picture your day as you want it to roll.
- Movement – get the tingles going in your body while you bop about to a happy tune.
- Mirror Work – do your affirmations whilst looking yourself in the eye.
- Reading – pick up one of your favourite books that reminds you of how awesome life is.
- Cards – pull an oracle or affirmation card to get some universal guidance.
- Exercise – yoga, run, walk, anything that makes you feel alive.
- Nature – get connected by sitting and just being in the garden or looking out.
- Tech Free – allow yourself the first couple of hours of the day to be tech free.
- Journaling – write out how you're feeling, what your purpose is, how you desire today to be.
- Listen – have a favourite speaker, podcast or book playing while you prepare for the day.

---

"It takes work to create inner peace."
*Donna & Cheryl*

---

### Evening Practice Ideas

- Switch off – decide a time you set aside work, ideally a couple of hours before bed.
- Prepare – get to-do lists out of your head and onto paper, also a couple of hours before sleep.
- Decisions – check your next day diary, decide clothes, food plan, etc. all way before bed.
- Relax – prepare your body for bed with a relaxing bath, salts and a candle.
- Stretch – some gentle yogic stretching and focused deep breathing.
- Daily Reflection – journal out any thoughts on the day, gratitudes and miracles.
- Visualisation – picture yourself in your life when you've achieved your big goals.
- Intention Setting – decide how great your next day is going to be.
- Meditation – five-twenty minutes to tune in to you and let the day go.
- Subconscious Meditation – listen as you sleep soundly.

The list above is for inspiration. Each day for you may be different so after you've experimented with the list and have a feel for the ones you most enjoy, create your favourite framework and work on getting consistent with that. Set the intention to practise even one thing in the morning and one thing in the evening then you can build and layer up from there.

## TIME TO KEEP IT REAL

Head over to your Book Resources at www.therealyoumethod.com/book-resources now and you're going to plan out your Morning and Evening Practice as it can make it easier to have it to hand as you get used to building this into your routine.

Journal on what works, what feels good and what you want to tweak.

Also note the differences to your energy, happiness and stress levels as you implement them to see what shifts you observe.

**Donna**

I'm holding this baby boy and looking at him as he's greedily guzzling his bottle of milk. He smells absolutely divine, that smell that babies have; I heard someone once call it Baby Chanel... it's so true. Beautifully intoxicating. He looks up at me with these huge brown eyes and he's trying to grin while sucking at his bottle and the milk dribbles down the side of his chubby cheeks. I have a feeling of love in my chest that is so huge, it feels like it's going to pop. I squeeze him in just a little bit closer and tell him how much I love him as I sit and cry big, fat happy tears.

## BE BRAVE ENOUGH TO DREAM

By the time this actually came true, I had been picturing it in my mind for four years. That's how long it took for the miracle who is our son Kaleb to appear in our lives. For anyone who has experienced the desire to have a baby, you'll know how excruciatingly painful and joyful the journey can be. I had always said I would never have children and when Neil and I got married, the plan was it would just be the two of us. But I realised as soon as I was married and for the first time in my life, I had a different kind of inner peace that I hadn't experienced before and I just knew I was ready to become a parent. I remember ringing Cheryl who was the first person I told, from a baby shop. I went there to test myself, to see if I would start hyperventilating. When I didn't, I knew I had to tell her.

"I'm in a baby shop and I'm imagining buying stuff for our baby, and I'm not coming out in a rash," I said slowly.

"Oooohhh..." she said slowly. This was as much news to her as it was to me. "And how do you feel?"

"Happy."

"Good – what happens next then?"

What did happen next was a four-year journey of various pills, procedures, prodding, injecting, lots of information relating to 'unexplained infertility' and two heart-breaking miscarriages. It was tough. As a control freak you like to be in charge of when things are happening and what the outcome is but this was a whole new ballgame. I realised very early on in the process that this would be all consuming if I allowed it. Meeting with doctors who deal in 'reality', stats and side effects rather than dreams, visions and feelings meant that I needed a whole new strategy to get through whatever was going to come.

I wanted to enjoy these processes because I knew they were happening to me for a reason and there was a really great prize at the end of it. For me, it wasn't an option to sit around and be miserable about the fact that it wasn't happening naturally or panic that my body wasn't working like it 'should'. I looked at it like this great, exciting project that would have different phases to it and along the way I would learn so much about my body and the process of how babies actually happen.

Whatever it took, however long or hard it was, I was all in. I was 100% committed to the outcome of having a family and I would do whatever I could at my end to hold up my side of the deal. I ate well, gave up alcohol for big chunks of time, trained hard or stopped training depending on what was needed, did acupuncture, took supplements... you name it. If I was told it would improve our chances of conceiving – I was all over it. I had a newfound awe and love for my body and what it could do. I was constantly astonished as I would learn more about its capabilities and I gained a respect for it that I would love all women to have. Having been so focused on what size my body was most of my life, here I now was, asking it to build a baby from scratch and getting her to jump through all kinds of hoops in the process. Our bodies are nothing short of miraculous.

> *"I let go of my need to control and allow The Universe to do her thing."*
>
> — GABBY BERNSTEIN

I stepped back from some big responsibilities at work because I wanted to reduce my exposure to stress and I already had a big job. This was huge for me to do. It felt like a massive decision because I felt like I was prioritising myself which isn't the most natural thing in the world for a woman with Imposter Syndrome. My faith and knowing that I was on a journey to having a baby outweighed any fear or ego that comes along with the Imposter.

I was completely and utterly dedicated to our vision of having a family.

## ENERGISE YOUR VISION

Whilst I took every step possible to have the best self-care routine and to take care of my mind and body like I had never done before, I spent time every single day in my vision. It was so important to me that this feel so real, so inevitable, that no matter what words flowed from the mouth of a consultant or whether there was a blue line on a pregnancy test, I would not be swayed from the knowledge that my baby was on its way to me. I didn't know from where, I didn't know when he was coming, but I knew he was on his way.

I would lie in bed each morning and picture myself going into the baby's room and seeing him stood up in his cot. I would picture going to nativity plays at school. I would think about where we would go on holiday. Through the day I would close my eyes and imagine sitting with a baby on my knee as I read him a story. At night before I would go to sleep, I would get my Hubby in on the action and we would talk about things we were looking forward to so that we both went to sleep with excited butterflies in our stomachs.

We would think about practicality as we got our new cars and work out if buggies would fit in the boot. We even bought a bigger bed because we knew we would need more room for Saturday morning snuggles. In the bed shop we both lay on the bed and imagined having the baby in the middle and we couldn't stop smiling thinking about what music we would play for him to listen to. We consciously embodied being a parent as we knew that this would be our best chance to have the thing we most wanted, happen in reality. We also wanted to create the physical space in our lives to let The Universe know we were ready and willing.

When you want something – when you really want something – you get to decide how committed to that thing you are. Not to how it happens, but to the result that you want. It's about you believing in it before you see it. About you deciding each day you wake and at each point of you being tested, if you're showing up as if it's a done deal or if you live from a place of doubt, uncertainty and fear.

---

"You get to be radically committed to your vision and create unwavering, unshakeable faith in it and you."
*Donna & Cheryl*

---

And you will be tested. There will be obstacles... this is life! Of course, there were days when I felt sadness, worry and confusion. We're all human, it's part of our design to feel these emotions. But for me, I didn't want to build momentum on those feelings. I wanted all the momentum and energy to be in the vision of what we desired our life to be. If someone else got pregnant, it didn't make me sad, it showed me that was possible for us too.

Anything is possible when you believe it. Your job is to build your faith in that vision. To have a daily practice of being in your vision, making decisions from that place and creating unbreakable and unwavering knowing that this is meant for you. When you do that, the whole Universe will conspire to support you in your dreams.

All you have to do is be brave enough to dream them.

## CHAPTER SUMMARY

- The Universe will send you tests to see how much you really want your goals.
- Your words create your world so choose them wisely.
- Hand over your white-knuckling and control to The Universe and let it take the strain while you stay blissed out in your faith that what you want is being worked out.
- Use your Five Steps to Come Back Home when you're out of alignment.
- Create your high vibe daily with practices that work for you and make it non-negotiable.
- Energise your vision not your fears and build momentum in what you want to see manifest. Do it every single day.
- Anything is possible and you don't have to worry about how it will happen; just be brave, dream big and have faith.

**My aha moment from this chapter is:**

# 11

# OUR WISH FOR YOU

> *"You've always had The Power my dear, you just had to learn it for yourself."*
>
> — GLINDA THE GOOD WITCH, WIZARD OF OZ

We are so honoured that you have taken this journey with us. It's a journey you will take every single day in this experience called your life and we hope you now feel you have more tools available to you to be able to grab that beautiful life with both hands. And you know it doesn't have to end here with us. Hell no, you're stuck with us now!

You have your Book Resources at www.therealyoumethod.com/book-resources and you can be with us for daily inspo and life lessons on Instagram and Facebook @nowisyourtimeto. If you're ready to go *all in* (and be stuck with us forever!) then you can join us in *The Real You Online* coaching programme where we are Live with you every single month. All the info you need is on your Book Resources page.

Now know this…

You don't need to be, do or have anything else to be happy. You can choose to be happy right now, right where you are. You are exactly where you need to be. You don't need to change anything about yourself to love yourself – you have permission to love yourself exactly as you are in this moment. Stop waiting for some major life event or to be in a fear free zone; you just have to decide that you're ready and then take inspired action, one step at a time.

This is just about you constantly expanding and discovering more of what you already are and becoming the best version of you. That will keep unfolding and you will keep discovering more layers of yourself so enjoy the journey rather than racing to get to some destination where you're done. You're never done and that's ok. It would be boring! And look what you've already achieved wearing the masks and the armour… just imagine what you're going to be able to do without it. This is what the world needs and is waiting for!

Don't waste one more moment of your precious time here keeping yourself small to keep everyone else happy. No more compromising on what you want your life to be. Stop playing it safe worrying that it might go wrong. Quit avoiding being visible and talking about your ambitions just in case someone thinks you're too big for your boots. Go running headfirst into your life, arms wide open, singing at the top of your lungs, laughing until your sides hurt and believing in miracles.

Be proud of the woman you already are and the woman you continue to become. Show off your flaws because they add up to the sum total of the incredible human being that is you. You are a one off, totally unique, complete original and there will never be another you. How amazing is that? Stand in your power and own it, this is your Becoming and you get to do it your way.

If our stories in this book have shown you anything, we hope it's that there is nothing special about us. If two middle aged women from the North East of England can start living the life of their dreams despite all of the odds, then you can too. There's no need to wait for the perfect time, perfect circumstances or perfect bank balance – perfect doesn't exist. Now is always the right time to get conscious and say 'YES' to all of your desires.

Everything you want is waiting for you. You deserve to experience all of the incredible things that your heart desires. You can have it all and don't let anyone else tell you differently. You are the CEO of your own life and you get to dream BIG. To top it off, you have the love and omniscient power of The Universe on your side. You can manifest the life of your dreams as soon as you decide that you are worthy of it and we hope that by now, you believe in *you* as much as we do. It's time to live into the infinite, limitless potential that you are and claim it.

Now Is Your Time to *be* **The Real You**.

Love and hugs,

Donna & Cheryl xx

# RESOURCES

We have created Book Resources to help you **Become The Real You** so make sure you grab them!

www.therealyoumethod.com/book-resources

Come join your free private **Become The Real You** Facebook community for our book readers where we will be connecting, supporting you and building this movement of incredible women who are ready to become the best versions of themselves and stand in their power.

The journey is so much more fun together.

Visit: www.facebook.com/groups/becometherealyou

# SOCIAL MEDIA

**INSTAGRAM:**
@nowisyourtimeto

**FACEBOOK:**
@nowisyourtimeto

**LINKEDIN:**
https://www.linkedin.com/company/now-is-your-time/about/
https://www.linkedin.com/in/donna-elliott-nowisyourtime/
https://www.linkedin.com/in/cheryl-lee-now-is-your-time-to-com/

**YOUTUBE:**
www.youtube.com/c/NowIsYourTime

**WEBSITE:**
www.nowisyourtimeto.com

**Contact Information**

For speaking enquiries, coaching programme information or any other help, please email hello@nowisyourtimeto.com

# ACKNOWLEDGEMENTS

Since day one of our hairbrained scheme to leave our corporate careers behind and embark on a voyage with no map to set up our own business, we have had an insane amount of love and support. Whilst our mission was strong, we know we would not have made it to this point without having been guided, encouraged, hugged or told to shut the fuck up and get on with it, by these people.

**Donna**

Thank you to my biggest cheerleaders, my parents Dorothy and Ken, for telling me my whole life that I could do anything I wanted to as long as I tried my best. You've always shown me complete, unconditional love and I hope I've made you proud because you both make me proud every day.

My little sister Kelly, the Louise to my Thelma... thank you from the bottom of my heart for walking in that night and for knowing who I was when I had no idea who I was any more. Thank you for kicking me up the arse, believing in our vision even when we questioned ourselves and for trusting that we could actually do this. You will always be the Hobnob to my Rich Tea.

Neil, I told you when I met you that I wasn't easy to live with and I'm pretty confident I've managed to maintain that statement. Setting up our business and writing our book has been a pretty huge undertaking and I've lost my shit many times over but I love you more for always seeing the best in me and for being as all in as we were on this crazy adventure.

Kaleb, thank you for making me feel extraordinary. Having you come into our life has made me more than a Mam. You've made me want to be a better person, you make me want to leave this world a better place and you make me want to show you that you can do anything in this life that you set your mind to. Thank you for stretching me, for teaching me and for showing me love that is simply indescribable. You're my hero.

**Cheryl**

Thank you to my Mam for supporting my dream and helping me to get where I am today. It means the world to me to have your encouragement and belief. Your strength and determination have shown me how to be the woman I am today.

Dad, I know you're at the biggest and best AC/DC gig in the sky and I feel your presence always spurring us on. I know you see the things we achieve and I know how much you would have bloody loved it.

To my hubby, Graham, thank you for putting up with the long hours, the risks we took to get here and for telling me to go for it. You make my world a safe place and I love you for all that you do for us.

My gorgeous daughter, Hollie, thank you for being not only the best daughter in the world ever, but also for being our Girl Friday in the business and helping us to serve our clients each day. You make me so proud to see the woman you are becoming and I am honoured to be your Mam. The legacy you're creating with us will live on through you... and Kaleb!

**From Both of Us**

A mahousive thank you to our epic team who keep us sane, work so hard and always hold the vision of what we are here to do in your hearts and minds. We couldn't do it without you.

To all of the women out there past and present, showing up, bringing your whole selves into the world with vulnerability, love and a ton of gumption – thank you for being the leading lights this world so needs.

We have the best cheerleaders in our girlfriends who have kept reminding us that we can do it. Thank you all for holding us to our vision. You know who you are – we love you, ladies!

Danielle Macleod, we are forever grateful for the rocket fuel. Thank you for making it all seem possible.

Our gorgeous Coach, Niyc Pidgeon, thanks for showing us what was possible, how to run a business, have a greater impact in the world and how to create the life of our dreams. You rock, lady.

Dr. Erin Fall Haskell, you are the most badass spiritual babe we know. You changed our lives and we love you.

Thank you to The Universe for bringing us together, for putting this book in your hands and for always guiding us to our highest good.

To each and every one of you in our movement, thank you for being brave, for trusting us and for making the world a better place by shining your beautiful light more brightly. You are way more than enough and you are *loved*.

# ABOUT THE AUTHORS

Donna Elliott & Cheryl Lee are mindset coaches and the founders of Now Is Your Time, a global movement helping women to break free from self-doubt and to live a life of happiness, balance and inner confidence.

Their signature methodology, The Real You™, empowers women in their coaching programmes to transform their old stories, limiting beliefs and Imposter Syndrome to reclaim their power and start playing all out in life.

After successful corporate leadership careers, they are now dedicated to showing women how to become the best version of themselves and to create a life overflowing with purpose, self-love and abundance.

Best friends and Soul Sisters, they hope by keeping it real and talking openly about their life experiences, other women will feel free to do the same and ditch the guilt and mental shackles of low self worth and discover they are already enough.

They speak at global brands such as the BBC, American Express, Adobe and to groups all over the world about the power of mindset mastery to achieve personal and business success.

Both live by the beach in the North East of England with their families, which is their happy place.

facebook.com/nowisyourtimeto
instagram.com/nowisyourtimeto

Printed in Great Britain
by Amazon

25662832R00126